HERTFORDSHIRE CASEBOOK

A reinvestigation into murders and other crimes

Paul Heslop

The
Book
Castle

For Kathryn

By the same author

The Job – 30 Years a Cop

The Walking Detective

Old Murders and Crimes of Northumberland and Tyne & Wear

Bedfordshire Casebook

First published August 2006 by
The Book Castle
12 Church Street
Dunstable
Bedfordshire LU5 4RU

ISBN 1 903747 70 8
ISBN 978 1 903747 70 4

Designed and typeset by Caroline and Roger Hillier
The Old Chapel Graphic Design

Printed by Print Solutions Partnership, Wallington, Surrey

Foreword

by Nick Cook

Buy this book and you are buying much more than a collection of crime stories linked by an accident of geography.

First, you are buying a lifetime's experience in the area of crime and punishment. Creative writing teachers frequently urge their students to "write about what you know". Paul Heslop has certainly has done that. His career began as a constable on the beat in 1960s Newcastle and culminated as a detective inspector in Watford, dealing with all types of crimes and specialising in child protection and domestic violence. In between lies 30 years' police experience, all of it at the 'sharp end' of the job.

Second, you are buying Paul Heslop's ability to tell a good story, which he unfolds with a novelist's skill and an expert's eye for detail.

Not that this book is merely a haphazard collection of Hertfordshire crimes. It is much more than that. These stories clearly illustrate the evolution of crime and punishment over the last century and a half. They start in Victorian and Edwardian Hertfordshire, a time when the mentally ill were officially labelled imbeciles, and a cancelled coronation celebration caused major riots. They end with the apparently motiveless murder of a retired Colonel in 2004, in the 'quintessential' village of Furneux Pelham.

Finally, you are buying judgement, a feature of which is The Verdict on whether justice was done, given after consideration of the facts as seen through the eyes of a former detective.

In an age when crime has recently replaced romance as the most borrowed fiction in public libraries, I can thoroughly recommend this book. Every case is painstakingly researched and presented in authoritative, entertaining and hugely enjoyable detail.

Nick Cook is a free-lance journalist specialising in health and safety, and environmental issues. He teaches creative writing in Hertfordshire and is President of the Verulam Writers Circle.

The Author

Paul Heslop is a former policeman who served in two police forces, Newcastle upon Tyne City Police (later Northumbria) and Hertfordshire Constabulary. He joined the Newcastle force in 1965, in the days when coppering was done on foot, supervised by patrol sergeants and inspectors, and on-street contact with the public was seen as an essential ingredient in policing.

In a career spanning over thirty years Paul served in CID, Special Branch and Regional Crime Squads, as well as uniform duties. As a detective he was directly involved in the investigation of murder and other serious crimes, including robbery, sexual offences, child abuse and domestic violence, as well as routine work. His Regional Crime Squad secondment in the South-East extended into London and the Home Counties.

Since retirement from the force in 1995 Paul has become a successful writer. His autobiography, an account of his walk 'the length of Britain' and two books on 'old crimes' in the North-East and Bedfordshire have been published. His work for newspapers and magazines includes such diverse topics as crime, local history and walking, as well as features on health and safety. He is an ardent fellwalker and lives in the Lake District.

Contents

I

BENINGTON 1871
The Killing of Police Constable Benjamin Snow 1
The First to Die *Shenley 1824* **PC Grainge** 12
Stevenage 1857 **PC Starkins** 14
Aldbury 1891 **On a Dark and Stormy Night** 15

2

A BITTER TASTE
Leavesden 1899 **The Case of Mary Ann Ansell** 19
"A mental degenerate" 28

3

WATFORD 1902
The Coronation Riot 31
"Hot-foot from slumdom" 43

4

RICKMANSWORTH 1911
"With very great brutality" **The Charles Coleman Case** 45
The Execution of Charles Coleman 54
Waltham Cross 1914 **The Last Execution** 55

5

BRICKET WOOD 1917
The Shooting of Janet Oven 59

6

Redbourn 1921
"I didn't hardly know what I was doing!" **Donald Litton – Child, Killer** 69
"A judge knows nothing..." 82

7

The 'Kid Gloves' Murder
Near Leverstock Green 1956 **Two Murder Hunt 'Firsts'** 85
Potters Bar 1955 **Murder on the Golf Course** 93

8

Marshalls Heath 1957
The Murder of Anne Noblett 97
Brookmans Park 1986 *"Rape is a natural thing for a man to do"* 107

9

Stocking Pelham 1969–70
The Kidnap and Murder of Muriel McKay 111
Hemel Hempstead 1990 *"An offence of great gravity"* 124

10

Hoddesdon 1970
The 'Red Mini' Murder 127

11

The Bovingdon Bug
Graham Young, the Bovingdon Poisoner, 1971 139
Freed to Kill 153

12

An Appallingly Dangerous Man
Nomansland 1977 **The Murder of Janie Shepherd** 155
Early Release from Detention 169

13
"With Considerable Courage"
Hemel Hempstead 1988 **The Murder of PC Frank Mason** 171
"Not afraid to do his duty" **PC Frank Hulme** 181

14
A Dastardly Crime
Ashridge Park 1988 **The Murder of Joan Macan** 185
Furneux Pelham 2004 **Murder without Motive?** 193

Postscript
"If we are to abolish the death penalty..." **Crime and Punishment** 197

Bibliography 202

Stocks and scold's seat, Brent Pelham

Let the punishment fit the crime

'Under every consideration I have given to your iniquitous case, it is my painful bounden duty to let you know that mercy in this world cannot be extended to you. Lose not a moment, I beseech you, in employing those few hours which you have left to live in hearty prayers and repentance for the dreadful crime you are now about to expiate by death.'

These were the solemn words of Justice Dallas at the Hertfordshire Assizes in July, 1817, addressed to the young man who stood before him, 18-year-old William Moles, who was charged with 'feloniously setting fire to a stack of wheat, "whereby the said stack and several carts, horses and other property amounting to upwards of £1,000 belonging to John Farr, were consumed" '.

William Moles was indeed guilty of arson, an act of retribution against a former employer, local farmer Mr Farr who, the previous April, had dismissed him from his service after Moles' alleged 'improper behaviour'. Moles admitted the charge, saying that he had set fire to the stack one morning, though whether he intended the consequences, which included the deaths of two or three horses, is doubtful. On 7th August, 1817, William Moles was taken to Weston, where he lived, on a cart, sitting on his coffin. There he was hanged from an oak tree, close to his mother's house. 'The novelty of such a scene drew together a great number of spectators'. One can only hope that they were satisfied at seeing justice dispensed and, if they were, that they considered the punishment meted out to young William Moles was merited.

Benington 1871

The Killing of
Police Constable Benjamin Snow

Benington, near Stevenage, is largely unchanged over the years. Anyone living in Victorian times, if they could visit Benington today, could still enjoy the peace of St Peter's parish church, or take a drink at The Bell public house just down the road. But one thing has changed. When a privileged few owned the land, the working class and peasants were forced by law to keep away. Poaching was the crime of the 19th century.

Not surprisingly, there were those who, often through necessity, committed trespass to shoot and snare and steal the animals their better-off peers owned. Poaching was a serious offence, and gamekeepers were employed to protect stocks. One might have had sympathy with poachers, most of whom took game to feed starving families and, if caught, could be transported or hanged. Such extreme measures were prevalent by, say, the late 1700s, although, let it be said, there were still plenty who could not afford to buy food and so took to poaching for the same reason as their forefathers.

In those less travelled times it was normal for policeman and poacher to be acquainted, with a kind of 'cold war' prevailing between them. Gamekeepers and poachers were often armed, whilst the lone bobby, the man expected to enforce the law, was not. At Benington, Constable Benjamin Snow and known poacher John Chapman knew one another right enough. What's more, Chapman was wanted on two warrants for poaching offences. One was held by Inspector Oliver at Buntingford. The other, as Constable George Williams, of Walkern, would testify, was issued in November, 1865. He, PC Williams, held that warrant and together with PC Snow had tried on occasion to execute it at Chapman's home at Luffnel, about four miles from Benington. To no avail, and Chapman, well aware he was a wanted man, disappeared. But, in January, 1871, PC Williams got wind that Chapman was in the Benington area again.

At noon on Tuesday, 10th January, armed with the information passed to him from PC Williams, PC Snow set forth from his police house in Benington to patrol his beat and, no doubt, keep a weather eye open for the elusive John Chapman. It seems that through neglect or choice he did not take his staff. It would be a fateful and short excursion, for when PC Snow returned home about an hour later he had injuries to his head, aparently not serious, but resulting in his death that very night. The tragic events that took place that afternoon would result in the arrest of John Chapman on a charge of murder, and the issues that ensued were twofold: whether it was he, Chapman, who inflicted the fatal injury on PC Snow; and whether PC Snow, in seeking to apprehend him without having the warrant in his possession, was acting within the law and, if he wasn't, could he, Chapman, be guilty of murdering him when he refused to be arrested?

Giving evidence at the inquest at The Bell two days later, PC Snow's distraught wife, Mary Ann, told the court that her husband had left home at twelve o'clock to make the 'point' at Sacombe Pound, that is to meet other policemen, which was normal procedure. When her husband returned a few minutes before one o'clock she could tell by his face there was something the matter. 'What, Polly, I don't know, dear,' he said, and then she noticed blood on his face and shoulder. She also saw a cut on his head, and he seemed confused. 'Enemy got the gun and run away,' he said, then he went upstairs where she helped bathe his head before he went to bed and fell unconscious.

The Bell public house, Benington

Dr Herbert Hodges, who attended PC Snow, told the inquest that he could not give satisfactory evidence as he had not yet conducted a post mortem on PC Snow's body. Consequently the inquest was adjourned to the following Monday, the day of the funeral. It would be held in Benington parish schoolroom, but before then events took a turn when John Chapman was arrested in London.

It followed enquiries by Inspector John Reynolds, of Stevenage, who had been aware of the warrants and the possibility of Chapman being in the Benington area. Later, at Chapman's trial, he would say that he had instructed PC Snow to apprehend Chapman, but to get assistance. Insp Reynolds learned of 'foul play' on the night of PC Snow's death and went to see the constable at his home, by which time

3

PC Snow had died. The following day he informed the Metropolitan Police that PC Snow had been murdered, allegedly by John Chapman. When Sergeant Turner of the Met arrested Chapman at Wood Green, Chapman said, 'I was at Benington. I have nothing further to say.' Chapman, a married man with five children, was taken to the Shire Hall, Hertford and charged with the murder of PC Snow. At the Wood Green address police found a gun and barrel, in two pieces, along with shot and powder. They also found a dead duck. Ever the poacher.

The adjourned inquest at the schoolroom was crowded with the good people of Benington. Chapman was brought from Hertford, but not allowed to witness proceedings, a strange situation when a man was accused of murder. By this time Dr Hodges had conducted the post mortem in PC Snow's house. Testifying, he said that when he was called to the house on the fateful day PC Snow was in bed, but had managed to sit up. The doctor found a large contusion on the left side of his head. There was a great deal of blood under his scalp, which was 'puffy'. The external wound was less than one inch long, more like an abrasion. It seems PC Snow's replies to the doctor's questions were indecipherable, that he could only be understood when saying 'Yes sir', and 'warrant'. Dr Hodges put this down to concussion. He remained with PC Snow for an hour and a half, and 'having done for him all that was possible' he left. When he returned at a quarter to midnight PC Snow was dead. He was 32, married with three children. It seems the doctor did not realise the extent of his internal injuries, but then he did not have the benefit of X-ray equipment or other hospital facilities.

The post mortem examination revealed that there was 'coagulated blood and smashed muscle' beneath PC Snow's scalp. There were two centres of bruising on the left side of his head. From this Dr Hodges deduced that two blows had been struck. The skull was fractured, and the bone slightly depressed, although insufficient to indent upon the brain. However, there was a mass of coagulated blood pressing onto the brain from the left to the right side of the head, and this was the cause of death. Dr Hodges went on to describe more technical detail, before adding that the wounds to the head must have been caused by a blow rather than a fall, 'I imagine by some blunt instrument.' The butt of a gun might make such a wound, he said. It remained for others to put events together, of PC Snow's movements that afternoon. The first to do so was Robert Blaxill.

Mr Blaxill lived in Benington. He was a roadman. He was breaking up stones on the road, about a mile and a half from PC Snow's house, when he saw the constable at about five past twelve. PC Snow was walking towards Whempstead, and Blaxill asked him the time. About three quarters of an hour later he saw him again. PC Snow spoke to him three or four times, but he was unable to understand him. The policeman held a handkerchief to his left ear, and Mr Blaxill asked him if he had earache. PC Snow replied, 'I have got shot.' He then walked off towards his home, still wearing his hat. When asked by the jury if he had heard a shot, Blaxill said that he had not. We can assume PC Snow went home, and that Blaxill did nothing to help a man who had told him he had been shot, even though he had not been.

Inspector Reynolds' endeavours on the morning after PC Snow's death were creditable. He was out at daylight, making enquiries from which he learned that Chapman had been seen going down Bourne Lane, and that he was followed by PC Snow. The inspector went down the lane and discovered signs of a struggle between two people, which he was able to deduce because snow lay on the ground and he could clearly distinguish the marks of a pair of good boots, such as would be worn by PC Snow, and a pair of old mended boots with hob nails. Of the latter, in the right boot the nails formed a zig-zag pattern in the centre, and there were distinctive nails in the heel. Further along the lane he saw signs of another struggle, with the same footmarks. He then traced the marks of the person wearing the 'mended boots' towards Green End. The length of the strides made it apparent that he was running away, and further on other marks showed that the wearer had stopped and turned round, possibly to see if anyone was coming. Further on again he was able to deduce that the wearer of the boots was splayfooted, as he had seen Chapman was. He followed the footprints for a mile and a half, to a public footpath.

When Chapman was arrested by Sergeant Turner of the Metropolitan Police, he put on a pair of boots which were later handed to Insp Reynolds, along with the barrel and stock of the gun taken from Chapman's home. Insp Reynolds examined the boots and said they corresponded with the footprints he had discovered in the snow when he had searched the area. Since the officer was unable to provide casts of footprints in the snow, and was unable to provide photographs, his testimony would have surely been received with some caution. Assuming he was telling the truth, it was the best he could do in the circumstances.

The next witness was James Gilbey, 'an intelligent looking and respectably attired lad' of about sixteen years of age. He lived at Benington and was a farm labourer. His testimony was vital to the case. He said that about 12 o'clock on the Tuesday he saw John Chapman cross Combe's field and step on to the road that leads from Whempstead. Gilbey was with a labourer called William Warner. Chapman asked Gilbey who the keeper was. Gilbey said, 'Master Palmer is gamekeeper to Mr Proctor.' Warner walked off, but Gilbey accompanied Chapman along the lanes and then said he was going up the hill. Chapman told him to wait where he was, as he was going somewhere 'to meet a man', saying that he wanted him to show him the way to Green End when he returned. Gilbey noticed that Chapman carried a gun, 'something like a barrel sticking out of one pocket and something like a stock in the other.' A few minutes after Chapman left him he heard a gun being fired. Gilbey walked in the direction Chapman had gone and met him coming back. Chapman then asked him the way to Green End. He said he would show him, and they walked along the lane, passing a garden with a man named Beadle working in it. Gilbey accompanied Chapman for 100 yards further, then told him the way to proceed. When Chapman was 'about a pole away', Gilbey saw PC Snow approaching. He said, 'Here's Mr Snow coming!' Chapman replied, 'That is, ain't it.' PC Snow passed Gilbey and went up to Chapman and he, Gilbey, saw the constable take hold of Chapman's jacket on the left side. Gilbey could not see any other person present. He then ran home 'very fast' because he was frightened.

William Beadle confirmed he was working in his garden that day, and that he saw a boy and a man go by, towards Green End. He did not recognise either, but when the boy came back alone he recognised him then as James Gilbey. He saw PC Snow going down the lane and the officer said to him, 'Do you know that man and boy as went down there?' Beadle said he did not. 'I will go down and see then,' said PC Snow. Beadle saw PC Snow again about ten minutes later, coming back, and walking at 'a middling pace'. PC Snow said, 'I am shot.' Beadle said, 'That's a bad job.' Beadle, like Blaxill, apparently did nothing to help a man who told him he had been shot.

At his trial at the Hertford Assizes in March, John Chapman pleaded Not Guilty to murder. The judge was Justice Hannen. Two warrants for poaching offences were produced: one by Inspector Oliver of Buntingford, the other by PC Williams. Insp Oliver said he did not know if PC Snow was a violent man, but he had heard he had a conviction for assault. PC Williams had also heard that PC Snow had been convicted of assault, but he did not know what it was. A policeman with a conviction for assault; this did not augur well for the prosecution's case.

Mr Clark, for the prosecution, told the jury that they must consider whether John Chapman was the man who did 'strike the blows' upon PC Snow, and whether he had resisted lawful arrest, on warrant, which the constable knew of but did not have in his possession. The law supposes malice, he said, a necessary ingredient on a charge of murder. It was the constable's duty to arrest him and he met with violent treatment that caused his death. It was wilful murder, he said. Mr Woollett, defending, disagreed, saying it was not the duty of a constable to apprehend a person upon a warrant that was in the possession of another constable.

That John Chapman was the man who inflicted the fatal wounds to PC Snow seemed certain. Gilbey and Warner had seen and spoken with Chapman near the time, and Gilbey had actually seen PC Snow take hold of Chapman's jacket. Dr Hodges had described the weapon as a 'blunt instrument', such as the butt of a gun. There was the evidence of Inspector Reynolds, the 'bootprints in the snow'. And Chapman had apparently said, 'I was in Benington.'

The issue wasn't who killed PC Snow, but whether Chapman did so 'with malice aforethought'. It was on a point of law that the verdict, and Chapman's fate, would hang – as hang he would, if convicted. In short, it was about whether or not PC Snow had the lawful authority to arrest him without having the warrant in his possession. The prosecution said it was addressed 'to all constables of the county' and that he, PC Snow, had known of and had seen the warrant in question, namely the one held in the possession of PC Williams. The judge intervened, citing a previous case, *Gaillard v. Laxton*. It had been laid down in court then that a warrant, although addressed to all constables, ought not to be executed unless by the person having it in his possession or was able to produce it upon being asked. The warrant should have been produced, said the judge.

Mr Clark countered this by arguing that, under the Poaching Prevention Act, it was lawful for a police officer to search or arrest any person whom he had cause to suspect had come from land where he had been unlawfully in search of game – as Chapman had undoubtedly been doing when he told Gilbey to wait for him. 'Cause to suspect' was all PC Snow required. Was this the reason the officer tried to arrest him, as he was entitled to do? No-one could say, but, having endeavoured to arrest Chapman, he received a blow that occasioned his death. Surely, he said, a charge of wilful murder was the right one.

Mr Woollett persisted with the 'warrant' argument, saying it was in English law that a constable was not empowered to arrest without a warrant not in his possession, 'and long might it be so for the safety of us all.' It had always been the law that a person being illegally arrested might resist, even to death. Such a person might be amenable to a charge of manslaughter, and no jury should convict him for murder. Chapman resisted, PC Snow

PC Snow's grave, Benington churchyard

persisted. No man could lament PC Snow's death more than he, and it was a painful thing to behold his young widow, deprived of her means of support. But the jury had it in evidence that PC Snow was of a violent turn of mind (his previous assault conviction). 'What amount of violence he may have used in endeavouring to arrest the prisoner no man could say.' Although Gilbey had seen PC Snow place his hand upon Chapman, that was all he saw, and what took place afterwards was a matter of speculation. If there were two scuffles there was a great amount of resistance, 'therefore exercise mercy in this case,' he implored the jury. When he sat down there was applause in the court. The killing of a policeman, it seems, and the level of guilt or otherwise of a man charged with murder was taking second billing to the oratorical abilities of two barristers.

Justice Hannen had the last word. He said the presumption of the law was that the prisoner had taken life intentionally, but the law considered that in some cases there may be extenuating circumstances. The provocation to resist in this case was that of a man about to lose his liberty, and the person who was about to deprive him, PC Snow, was not legally authorised to do so. The act was deprived of that essence of malice necessary to constitute murder. If Chapman had received illegal violence, and he resisted with violence, even to death, it amounted to manslaughter.

The Verdict

That John Chapman killed Constable Benjamin Snow is not in doubt. What might be is the verdict of the jury: were they right to find him guilty of manslaughter and not murder?

That PC Snow was acting in good faith and doing his job is not in doubt either. He knew there was a warrant in force for Chapman's arrest, and had been instructed to arrest him by his inspector, and to 'get assistance'. True, he was alone when he tried to arrest Chapman; but he had told his wife he was going to the point at Sacombe Pound, and it may have been to rendezvous with his colleagues, his 'assistance'. When, perchance, he came upon Chapman, he would hardly have passed him by.

Then again, the officer may have been acting under the Poaching Prevention Act, which empowered him to search Chapman, a known poacher, and arrest him on having reasonable cause to believe he had come from land where he had been in search of game. Couldn't he have been doing this very thing? Gilbey said he

The jury deliberated briefly before returning a manslaughter verdict. Justice Hannen: 'The jury have taken a merciful view. It would be a fearful thing indeed if men were to be allowed to suppose that, because a police constable sought to arrest them without a warrant, that they were justified in using such violence as had been used in this case.' He sentenced John Chapman to 15 years' hard labour. PC Snow was buried in the churchyard at St Peter's Church, Benington.

heard a shot, and saw the gun parts in Chapman's pockets, so you may be assured the constable would have seen them also. Maybe PC Snow wasn't acting with regard to the warrant at all. Why wasn't more weight attached to this by the court? Probably because it is for the prosecution to prove these things, and the only witnesses were PC Snow, who was dead, and Chapman, who would hardly be likely to support the prosecution's case.

The Judge said PC Snow, not having the warrant, was 'not legally authorised' to arrest Chapman. In days of poor transport and communication, one wonders what use warrants were if they could only be executed when in an officer's possession. All other policemen must pass wanted men by, then. Chapman was entitled to defend himself 'to the death', said defence counsel. PC Snow would have been better off ignoring Chapman's presence entirely if men in wigs were going to argue the toss in court later. As for Chapman, he didn't hang, but he didn't come out of this well either. Prisons in Victorian times were not like today's institutions, with televisions, access to drugs and early release. He was sentenced to 'hard labour'. He probably wished he'd hanged.

The First to Die

Shenley 1824 PC Grainge

On New Year's Day, 1824, James Grainge of Shenley Hill, a shoemaker, acting as a Special Constable, was the first Hertfordshire policeman to be murdered. The unlikely culprit was a doctor, Patrick Connolly, of Brighton.

Connolly had appeared at court for defamation of character and been ordered to pay £500 compensation. Rather than pay the money, or just as likely because he couldn't pay it, he went on the run and turned up at Rabley House, near Shenley, the home of Captain Nestor. When his whereabouts became known, the sheriff's officer, Thomas Watson, accompanied by an assistant and an attorney, went to Rabley House to arrest him. Mrs Brown, in charge of the house in Captain Nestor's absence, said she had not heard of Mr Connolly and refused to let the lawmen inside. One of them kicked the door, which shattered the glass, revealing Connolly who was standing in the hallway. Connolly thrust a braising iron, then a pitchfork, through the gap where the window had been, injuring Watson and his assistant. He then called out to a farm labourer to go and fetch a gun. As the law officers tried to break down the door, the labourer arrived with the gun, which he passed to a servant through a cellar window.

On New Year's Eve the local magistrate, having heard of the incident, swore in a number of special constables, which was normal procedure in those days. One of the specials was James Grainge, who demanded Connolly give himself up. Connolly refused, whereupon S/Con Grainge struck the door with an axe. Connolly responded by firing the gun, the shot striking S/Con Grainge in the arm. The injured officer was taken to the White Horse Inn for treatment. Connolly surrendered when reinforcements arrived, and he with others in the house were reportedly locked up in Shenley Cage for the night. At three o'clock the following day, after an operation to amputate his arm, James Grainge died at his home. Connolly escaped conviction for murder at the Hertford Assizes but was transported.

Shenley cage

Stevenage 1857 PC Starkins

The first regular Hertfordshire officer to be murdered was 25-year-old John Starkins. An officer with just a few months' service, PC Starkins was stationed at Stevenage. His murder was a dreadful crime, for which Jeremiah Carpenter, the accused man, was charged and acquitted.

Carpenter, a known thief, was suspected of stealing seed from his employers. He lived in a cottage near to where Stevenage police station now stands. On the afternoon of Friday, 30th October, 1857, PC Starkins was seen in a field near Carpenter's cottage. Half an hour later Carpenter arrived at the cottage in a dishevelled state, and PC Starkins failed thereafter to report to go off duty. A search was made for the officer, and on the Monday morning he was dragged from a pond 'with his throat cut so frightfully that his head was nearly severed from his body'. Jeremiah Carpenter and his brother were arrested for the crime.

The evidence, albeit circumstantial, weighed heavily against Jeremiah Carpenter. His clothes had gone missing and when found had parts cut away, and were impregnated with washing solution; his seed basket had been scrubbed but bloodstains and barley seed remained in the crevices. His knife had been washed but there was blood under the handle, and the blade matched the wounds to PC Starkins' body and his coat. Another officer, PC Quint, allegedly overheard Carpenter confess to the crime in the prison wagon, but this was disputed.

After hearing the evidence, the jury returned a 'not guilty' verdict, stating, 'We think there was great suspicion against the prisoner, but insufficient direct evidence for us to find a verdict of guilty'. PC Starkins was buried in St Michael's Churchyard, St Albans. Jeremiah Carpenter went back to live with his wife in their cottage, where they raised three daughters.

Aldbury 1891

On a Dark and Stormy Night

Aldbury, nestling in the lee of the Chilterns below Ashridge, is largely unchanged from the days when straw-plaiting provided a living for many of its residents. The medieval stocks and whipping post still stand by the duckpond, the old, timber-framed houses remain, as does the 18th-century Greyhound public house which, on a grim December day in 1881, became part of a tragic chain of events when the peace of the village was shattered by a double-murder.

It took place in a wood known as Aldbury Nowers, near Stocks, a large country house situated half a mile from the village. Like so many gruesome murders in those days, the issue was over poaching. The Stocks shooting rights had been let to Joseph Williams of Pendley, who employed two gamekeepers to patrol the estate. They were James Double, head keeper, and his deputy, William Puddephatt. The men took it in turns to patrol, usually with a helper, Joseph Crawley, also in Williams' employ. Puddephatt lived at nearby Stocks Cottage. Crawley had been a farm labourer; a native of Great Gaddesden, he too lived in the village.

On the night of Saturday, 12th December, 1891, Puddephatt and Crawley set off on patrol. They were armed with stout sticks. One can imagine the scene: the wind howling through the wood, the occasional glimpse of the moon – ideal conditions for poachers, who could make their way unseen, their gunshots unheard in the storm. But that night, Puddephatt and Crawley did not return. At eleven o'clock the next day their bodies were discovered in a field at the far side of the wood by James Double and a gardener named Willmore, who had gone searching for them. They had been battered to death and had lain for hours in the rain and their own blood. Willmore went off to Tring to inform Sergeant Page of the tragedy, whilst Double returned to

The Greyhound, Aldbury

Aldbury to arrange transport of the bodies to the Greyhound public house, where an inquest would be held. As Christmas loomed in this tiny community, two men going about their lawful duties had been brutally slain, their wives widowed. Puddephatt had five children, Crawley seven.

Two police forces were involved: Bucks County, who had charge of the criminal investigation – indeed Captain Drake, the Chief Constable, rode out on horseback to the scene of the crime – and Hertfordshire, who had the bodies and in whose territory the murdered men had lived and, as it happens, did the three men responsible for the crime. They were quickly identified, not surprising perhaps in

16

a small community and in times when few travelled about. Three renowned poachers, Frederick Eggleton, Charles Rayner and Walter Smith, all from Tring, had been seen the previous night, drinking in a number of local hostelries.

Smith, a labourer, was quickly arrested. He denied complicity, saying he had gone straight home from the Greyhound on the night in question, even saying 'goodnight' to PC Best, the village constable. Perhaps he did, but this would not have ruled him out from meeting up again with the others. It seems Eggleton and Rayner called on him on the Sunday, probably to flee with them, but his wife said he was still in bed. A reward of £100 was put on their heads. After being spotted in Tring and again near Wendover, they were arrested near Slough. They said they had read of the murders in the newspapers, and seeing that the descriptions of the suspects matched their own they had fled in fear of apprehension. They hid at Long Farm, near Slough, from where they emerged straight into the arms of a constable, who arrested them. Their sudden disappearance no doubt sparked certainty that they were guilty, which would not have helped their cause at the ensuing trial. Rayner had served twelve years as a soldier, so perhaps he was well acquainted with the rules of staying at large and looking after himself.

It was established that Smith was the man in possession of the gun on the night of the murder, and that he had thrown the broken stock into the canal. It was recovered by police. He admitted being in company with the others, including when they attacked the two gamekeepers, but insisted he left before murder was done. All three admitted they had encountered the gamekeepers in the wood that night. In his statement Smith said, 'We all three went to Aldbury Nowers wood in search of game. Rayner had the first shot and missed. I had the next and killed a hen bird, then Puddephatt and Crawley came to us and us three started off, but they flew in at us and Crawley said, "You bastard, I will kill you." We all five fought in the field for half an hour. We started to go but Puddephatt said, "Come on Joe, we

Aldbury

can take them." and Crawley said, "Knock the bastards down." There was a great struggle. The men were alive when I left.' Smith's evidence was accepted, perhaps to cement a conviction against the others. He was sentenced to 20 years' hard labour. Eggleton and Rayner were convicted of murder. The judge passed the only sentence he could. There were moves to have them spared the noose, as between them they had fourteen children whose welfare would fall on the parish if they were executed. It did no good: they were hanged on 17th March, 1892.

2

A Bitter Taste

Leavesden 1899

The Case of Mary Ann Ansell

As someone who had been a patient in the Asylum for Imbeciles, Leavesden, for four years, Caroline Ansell would have enjoyed few of life's pleasures. So she would have been pleased to receive an unexpected gift by way of a small parcel, which contained a cake. The parcel had been sent anonymously, which must have seemed strange. Nonetheless, the following day Caroline ate some of her cake, then kindly shared it with her fellow patients, some of whom immediately spat it out. But Caroline and Mary Smithers became seriously ill, and four other women who had eaten some cake also became ill, though less so. Caroline and Smithers were taken to the asylum infirmary. Caroline died the following Tuesday, 14th March, 1899.

Nor was this the only strange gift to come through the post for Caroline. A short time before she was the recipient of some tea and sugar, which she had tasted and discarded, saying it was 'bitter'. Then there was the letter she had received from her cousin Harriett: 'Dear Carrie, I now send these few lines to tell you that your father and mother is dead (*sic*). They died last week'. Caroline saw little of her parents, who lived in London. She replied to her cousin, asking to see the funeral cards, only to discover that the news was false. Her cousin sent her letter to Caroline's parents, who would have been as mystified as she as to who sent the letter about their 'deaths', and its purpose.

At the subsequent inquest, evidence was heard from Nurse Alice Felmingham, who was in charge of Ward 7, where Caroline was a patient. She confirmed that the previous Thursday Caroline had received the parcel containing the cake, which she had witnessed being opened. The 'cake' took the form of a piece of pastry, which 'looked like a jam sandwich'. Caroline had eaten some of it the following day, Friday, for her tea. On Saturday she felt quite ill, and the whites of her eyes had turned yellow. On Tuesday she was speechless and suffering from intense abdominal pains. That evening she died. She was twenty-six years old. Death was put down to peritonitis – inflammation of the peritoneum (the membrane lining the abdominal cavity).

The circumstances of Caroline's death, and the illnesses suffered by the other patients, not surprisingly aroused suspicion in the mind of the asylum Superintendent. Not unreasonably, he decided to call for a post mortem examination, for which he sought the written authority of the deceased's next of kin, Caroline's parents, who lived at Grays Inn Road, London. When Caroline's mother came to the asylum on the Thursday, accompanied by Caroline's sister Mary, she was told about the cake. She said she knew nothing of any cake, but would consult her husband about 'consent' regarding the post mortem. A letter subsequently arrived, signed 'W. Ansell' (Caroline's father), pointing out that Caroline had been under the care of the hospital for four years. Consent for a post mortem was denied.

Nevertheless, a post mortem was carried out, by Dr Alfred Cox, on the authority of the Coroner. Dr Cox told the inquest jury that there were signs that death had occurred through 'irritant poisoning' He had taken out the viscera – the organs of chest and abdomen – for examination, and sent them to Dr Thomas Stevenson of Guy's Hospital, a well-known analyst employed by the Home Office to investigate such cases. Dr Stevenson examined the viscera for traces of phosphorus, but found none. But phosphorus is rarely detected if

Leavesden Asylum
Photo: The Watford Observer

the victim survives three or four days after consuming it. Phosphorus tastes 'bitter', as had the tea and cake. He gave 'phosphorus poisoning' as cause of death.

The inquest was adjourned, but in the interim the wrapper which had contained the cake was found by police in the grounds of the asylum. It had a London postmark. Sergeant Stoten then went to the home address of Mr and Mrs Ansell, in London, and took possession of some letters. A Christmas card, found in Caroline's possession and in the handwriting of Mary, was handed to police by nursing staff. Handwriting, on the letter and the wrapper, the Christmas card and other documents, would become a telling feature in this investigation. Meanwhile, following information received concerning the examination of the viscera, police went to Great Coram Street, London, where they arrested Mary Ann Ansell, Caroline's sister, on suspicion of murder.

21

Mary was twenty-two. When charged with her sister's murder, she replied, 'I know nothing whatever about it. I am as innocent a girl as ever was born.' She admitted to police that she had sent Caroline the Christmas card, but denied writing any letters to her for months. So what made the police suspect she was the person who had sent the poisonous tea and sugar, and the cake? And what could have been her motive?

Mary had worked in service for Mr Maloney at 42 Great Coram Street, London, on and off for five years. Mr Maloney was insured by the Royal London Friendly Society, and it was practice for Mary to pay the premiums on his behalf to Mr John Cooper, an insurance agent. Doubtless seeking extra commission, Cooper had urged Mary to insure herself also. She had declined, but on 6th September, 1898, she declared she would insure the life of her sister, Caroline. They were fond of each other, she said, and in the event of anything happening to Caroline she, Mary, would like to be able to give her a respectable burial. She told Cooper Caroline worked at the Leavesden asylum – not that she was a patient there, in which case the insurance proposal would not have been accepted. She undertook to pay a shilling a month premiums. Caroline would have to live for six months for payment of half benefit, that is until 6th March, 1899, a year for full payment, in either case providing she died from natural causes. Any insurance payment in the event of Caroline's death would be made to Mary. Caroline died on 14th March, so half of the insurance money, £11.5s (£11.25), a considerable sum then, was due to Mary, who had kept up to date with monthly premiums. Mary, probably unwittingly, had sent the cake to poison her sister without knowing she would only receive half benefit.

On her sister's death, Mary wrote to Cooper. 'I now send these few lines to ask your advice, what should I do about my sister's insurance...?' Cooper replied, saying that if she took the insurance policy and certificate of death to the insurance company's branch office she would be paid. But no certificate of death was issued, as a post mortem examination had been decided upon. A few days later Cooper went to see Mary. He said he had discovered she had made a false statement, that he had discovered Caroline 'had been a lunatic at the asylum'. The insurance money would not be paid, although her premiums would be refunded. Mary told Cooper she had lost the insurance book. It may be noted that the letter, purporting to be sent to Caroline by Harriett Parish, began with the same words: 'I now send these few lines...', in the manner that Mary had opened her letter to Cooper.

Emily Noakes, who worked in a shop for her father, an 'oil and colourman', said that Mary Ansell had constantly called at the shop, which was situated near to where she (Mary) worked in service at Great Coram Street. She said about six months previously Mary had bought some phosphor paste, saying there were 'a great many rats' at her employers' home. She bought about four or five bottles in all. Mary's employer, Mrs Maloney, said that she had never sent her to buy any such thing. Yes, there were rats, a few, but Mary would catch them in traps. Mary also had her own cooking facilities, she said. Could it be she baked and sent her sister the cake?

A handwriting expert was called. In today's world of criminal investigation, experienced detectives are sceptical about such evidence. In Victorian times, it seems, such 'expert' opinion was held in high regard. Mr Thomas Gurrin gave his opinion on handwriting 'throughout the United Kingdom'. After examining all relevant documents – the address on the wrapping paper, the handwriting in the letter purporting to have been sent by Harriett Parish – against documents known to have been written by Mary, including the Christmas card, he was able to say that Mary's was the handwriting in every case, albeit some of it had been disguised. She had sent the fraudulent letter, she had written the address on the parcel. The inquest jury found that 'Caroline Ansell died from the effects of phosphorus poison, contained in the cake sent by Mary Ansell in order to obtain the insurance money...'. Mary was committed to the Assizes.

Mary Ansell stood trial at the Shire Hall, Hertford, the following July. Justice Mathew presided. In a 'firm and loud' voice she pleaded 'not guilty' to the murder of her sister. *The Watford Observer* reported that 'she regarded the witnesses with a somewhat sullen look, but otherwise seemed unmoved by what was taking place'. Evidence was given regarding the letter sent to Caroline, purportedly by her cousin Harriett, but, the prosecution inferred, in reality by Mary. Its purpose was clear: having taken out insurance on her sister's life, it was crucial to Mary's insurance claim that when Caroline died the hospital did not contact her parents — which they would not if they believed them to be dead. Such a course would have raised questions about her 'illness'. Mary wanted no fuss, just a death certificate to secure the insurance payout.

When the asylum authorities notified Caroline's parents of her death, her mother and sister Mary attended on 16th March. They requested a death certificate and were told they had to apply for one. A helpful porter wrote a letter on behalf of Mary, who posted it. But having regard to the number of patients who had been taken ill, notably Caroline and Mary Smithers, the doctor in charge suggested it would be best to hold a post mortem examination. Mrs Ansell said she would consult Caroline's father, to whom Mary said, 'Father, if I were you I would not let them have a post mortem.' Mr Ansell told her to write a letter on his behalf (he being illiterate), which was sent to the hospital, declining consent for a post mortem. But suspicion abounded, and the Coroner overruled him.

It was vital for the prosecution's case to prove death had been caused by phosphorus poisoning. No phosphorus had been found in Caroline's remains. Dr Stevenson had considerable experience in phosphorus poisoning cases. He told the court that when first consumed, phosphorus produces sickness and nausea and internal irritation. The patient would normally get over it in 24 hours, even seem quite well. But for the following two or three days the poison would act against the kidneys and liver, causing 'fatty degeneration'.

This would be accompanied by jaundice and acute pain. He gave other, specific medical evidence, supporting his view that Caroline had consumed phosphorus. She and others ate some cake, but where some spat it out others swallowed and became ill. Mary Smithers was fortunate to survive. It was reasonable for the doctor in the infirmary to diagnose peritonitis, having no cause to suspect Caroline had consumed phosphorus.

When nurse Alice Felmingham testified, the defence suggested illness in the asylum had been rife. A newspaper story was quoted: 'About fifty of the patients of the Leavesden Asylum are suffering from a mysterious disease believed to be enteritis or typhoid'. Was that accurate? 'I don't know about that because all the patients are isolated,' she replied. It would be astonishing for so many people to be seized by a disease of the same kind at the same moment. The other victims then testified, effectively ruling out any suggestion of an epidemic. All had eaten the cake; all had either spat it out or taken ill in some degree. Mr Gurrin, the handwriting expert, said handwriting on the exhibits was in every case Mary's. His testimony was challenged, but only slightly, on the manner of some of the lettering, and a suggestion that the paper used was common enough. Caroline's father told the court that Mary had urged him not to agree to a post mortem. He, too, had taken out an insurance policy for Caroline, but it had lapsed due to arrears in contributions. He had nothing to gain by Caroline's death.

Defence counsel 'struggled manfully to upset the evidence', and to suggest that the poor woman died of yellow atrophy of the liver. But that is a rare disease, which in any case causes shrinkage of the liver, whereas in this case the liver was normal size. Another point was that Mary said she had lost the insurance policy and book, an attempt, said the prosecution, to suggest she had not taken out insurance on Caroline's life.

At 1.15 the jury retired. They returned at 2.20 without reaching agreement. They complained that they were not in possession of all the documents (one of them was brave enough to ask, 'Can we have any refreshments, my Lord?') The judge ordered that they were given all the documents and told them to retire again. They did so, and returned again at 8 o'clock. The verdict was 'guilty'.

The judge put on the black cap. There could only be one sentence. 'It is impossible that this jury, as reasonable and conscientious men, should return any other verdict than guilty. It has been shown to their satisfaction that you deliberately took the life of your sister, an afflicted woman who never had been a burden to you, and who had the utmost claim upon your affection and compassion. You were

---

The Verdict

Motive is not a lawful requirement of proof in a crime trial. But motive, nevertheless, can be a vital ingredient in a prosecution's case. Who would wish to murder an inmate in an asylum for imbeciles, as the institution that held Caroline Ansell was unkindly called? Who would go out of their way to bake a cake, lace it with phosphorus and post it to a hapless victim? Mary Ansell, Caroline's sister, that's who.

For there can be no doubt that it was she, as she duly confessed when facing death. But was she alone in this enterprise? It's just that somewhere in this unfortunate story the author of these pages feels that there may be a missing ingredient. A lover. A conspirator. Someone who engineered 'Silly old Ansell' to take out life insurance on Caroline, her sister, send her poisoned tea and cake, falsely inform her of the deaths of her parents and, after Caroline's demise,

moved to perpetrate this terrible crime for the sake of this small sum of money you would receive on the policy of insurance. Never in my experience has so terrible a crime been committed for a motive so utterly inadequate. I feel bound to warn you that you must be prepared to follow your victim. Time will be allowed you, and I hope it will be employed in seeking mercy.' He sentenced Mary to death. As she turned to go down the steps she screamed out, and so did her mother. The judge then continued with the day's business, a civil action concerning a claim for alleged detention of goods near Potters Bar.

urge her father not to consent to a post mortem examination which would reveal the true cause of death. Did Mary Ansell alone really possess the guile to undertake such a well thought-out course of action? There is fleeting reference to such a 'missing ingredient'. In her prison cell it was reported 'she did not seem to have asked for the man she is supposed to have loved'. The sisters' parents said Mary and Caroline had always been friendly to each other; her father had never heard Mary breathe a single word of malice against Caroline. If there was 'a man' he wasn't charged, as he should have been, for he would have been equally guilty.

Mary Ansell alone stood trial. She killed her sister, but did she murder her? Or was she insane? Was the entire plot the brainchild of someone else? Without answers to these questions she should not have hanged. There is cause for concern over this case. Phosphorus isn't the only ingredient to leave a bitter taste.

"A mental degenerate"

The jury found Mary Ann Ansell guilty of murder. But at least two of them did so in the belief that she would not hang. The foreman of the jury, Charles Cusworth, of Bushey, was quoted as saying, 'I am deeply upset at seeing the decision of the Home Secretary to hang Mary Ansell. We had no idea she would really be hanged.' Another juror, Mr Wise, of Elstree, said, 'I fully expected she would be reprieved.'

If mercy wasn't to spare Mary, would another factor, insanity, do so? Medical opinion 'as to her brain' was sought. Dr Nicholson, on behalf of the Home Office, contended that the prisoner's relatives were tainted with insanity: her grandmother was subject to fits; the sister whom she killed was insane; her younger sister was a confirmed imbecile. Mary herself was known as 'Silly old Ansell'. He submitted a report stating that, 'I have come to the conclusion that Mary Ansell is a mental degenerate and ought not to be held responsible, based on hereditary insanity'. If there was an issue of insanity, why wasn't it brought up when it mattered — at the trial? Then we could have learned what the jury made of it. If she was insane she could not be guilty of murder. Meanwhile, as Mary awaited her fate, Dr Forbes Winslow, her legal representative, was not permitted to visit her in prison.

Members of Parliament signed a petition, and another with a thousand names of members of the public was presented asking for the Royal prerogative of mercy. The Home Secretary's response was: 'Having carefully considered all the circumstances, and having

RIGHT **Artist's impression of Mary Ansell's execution at St Albans prison,**
19th July, 1899
She was buried within the confines of the jail, and later interred in
St Albans cemetery.
The Watford Observer

caused special medical enquiry to be made as to the convict's medical condition by Dr Nicholson, visitor in lunacy, I have been unable to find sufficient grounds to justify Her Majesty to interfere with the due course of law'. Mary was doomed.

The final plea came from Mary's parents, who wrote to the Home Secretary pleading for their daughter's life. She had always been 'silly', and had never borne malice towards her sister. One can sympathise: of their four daughters, one had been killed earlier in a tragic accident, one had been murdered and now a third was to be hanged. They did not receive a reply. The day before the execution they went to see Mary, and spoke to her through the grill of her prison cell. Mr Ansell said afterwards that his daughter could not bring herself to believe she had got to die, saying, 'Can you forgive me, father?' He could. He did.

There remained the grim day of execution, Wednesday, 19th July. The venue: St Albans prison. The sun shone on a lovely morning. Soon after seven o'clock the crowds gathered. Bets were taken: would she be reprieved? By eight o'clock some 3,000 had gathered. People positioned themselves on the railway bridge and embankment, awaiting the appearance of the black flag which would signify that the execution had taken place. The hangman was James Billington. Mary was reported as 'calm' until the final walk to the scaffold, just thirty paces, before she was overcome. She prayed as she walked, and on the scaffold repeated after the Chaplain, 'Oh God, forgive this miserable sinner.' Billington moved her onto the centre of the trapdoor. 'That will do,' he told Mary. 'Now be brave.' Then he pulled a cloth cap over her head and tightened the strap around her dress. The drop was seven feet. Death was reported as instantaneous. They ran the flag up for the benefit of the crowd. The following Tuesday the Home Office announced that Mary Ann Ansell had made a full confession. She was buried within the precincts of the prison, but interred in St Albans cemetery in 1930.

3

Watford 1902

The Coronation Riot

The Coronation of a new monarch has always been a cause for celebration, and never more so perhaps than in 1902, for in May of that year the Boer War had ended and Saturday, 28th June was Coronation Day, marking a new beginning after Victoria's long reign. The good citizens of Watford, young and old, looked forward to the forthcoming celebrations: the children's sports day in Cassiobury Park, the band and the grand procession and, in the evening, the lighting of the bonfire.

Alas, as events would show, Watford would become a town of shame, following scenes of drunkenness, assault, the plundering of property, arson and malicious damage, when hundreds of men and women rioted, many of them ending up in jail. Yet the cause of the trouble was unavoidable, as the Coronation had to be cancelled due to King Edward VII having perityphlitis. Referring to the riot at Watford at the Herts Assizes on the Monday after a shameful weekend, Justice Phillimore said that he had hoped that a time of harmless merriment and joy might have accompanied the 'great festival', remarking that most of the country had 'borne so well the disappointment they had experienced through the cancellation'. Instead, the people of Watford had permitted themselves to indulge in riotous excess, so that the police had to be commissioned in order to keep the peace.

Commissioned to keep the peace, yes. Succeeded in keeping the peace, hardly. But failure to keep the peace did not lie at the door of the police. The fact was, on the night, the riotous crowds were too big and too determined to control, and the force of police was inadequate. Indeed, with the riot in full swing, half of Watford's force had to be dispatched to Hemel Hempstead, a town with a riot of its own.

Contracting perityphlitis, which we now know as appendicitis, was hardly the fault of the King. But the operation in those days was far from straightforward, and Edward was in serious risk of death. With the Coronation just days away, and the celebrations imminent, it was perhaps understandable that the Watford town council felt there was no choice but to cancel festivities. After all, as Mr Murphy, who opened proceedings at the ensuing court hearing, said, 'it would hardly have done for the nation to be celebrating the Coronation if at the same time His Majesty was in a coffin'.

The chairman of the town council was Francis Fisher, a local butcher. When he called the Coronation Committee together, all were agreed there was no option but to cancel festivities: the band, the procession, the old folks' dinner, the children's sports in Cassiobury Park, along with a Coronation shilling to each child, and the lighting of a giant bonfire. This would have been a bitter blow to the community in those post-Victorian days, but good citizens accepted the situation stoically. Not so the rougher element of the town, who had looked forward in no small degree to drinking the health of the newly-crowned King. The street decorations came down, but the bonfire remained in situ, with hopes that it would be lit quite soon. It was, but sooner than the council anticipated and not in the way they intended. Instead, the bonfire became the catalyst for the troubles.

By Wednesday of the week after the cancellation some of the local 'roughs' of Watford were still dissatisfied with the council's decision. The following morning, as Mr Fisher walked to his shop premises, he was hissed at, he being the one the rowdy element blamed for spoiling their fun. Rumours abounded; there was going to be trouble. The crowds began to gather. By 8 o'clock the police had turned out and

Edward VII

matters were in hand. But by 9 o'clock the crowd was so dense vehicles had difficulty in passing. The crowd thinned, but if the police thought all was going to be well they were mistaken, for instead of dispersing the mob moved down Market Street in the direction of the still-unlit bonfire. By 9.30, thousands of people were streaming through the approaches to the Harwoods Estate, where the bonfire was situated.

Beside the bonfire was a watchman's hut. The watchman was dragged from the hut and beaten, and even threatened with being thrown on to the bonfire. He fled, whereupon the mob threw the hut and some nearby fencing on to the pile, which was then lit. The crowd watched it burn, and someone expressed the sentiment that it was a pity Fisher himself was not upon it, and that he would soon be if he showed his face.

The town surveyor, Mr Waterhouse, arrived. He tried to reason with the crowd. In vain. Dr Hall went to his assistance and led him away to safety, along with Mr Fuller. Some of the mob followed, incensed at Mr Waterhouse's interference. They sought sanctuary at the first house they came to in Benskin Road, the home of Mr Locock and his wife and children. A few moments lapsed before they were admitted, during which they were pelted with stones and flints. When they were admitted into the house stones were thrown through the windows, much to the consternation of Mr Locock, who was obliged to move his wife and children to the rear for their own safety. Then the mob, still described as numbering 'thousands', but in reality probably hundreds, dispersed, and moved away to the High Street.

The mob's ire was now directed at Mr Fisher, and it was not long before a stone was thrown through a window of his shop. This was the signal for stone-throwing all round, and another stone was thrown, through the window of Mr Longley's drapery store. Mr Longley had anticipated events and had boarded up the lower part of the shop, which seemed only to incite the mob, some of who tore the barricade down. The police arrived in the form of four mounted officers. They charged into the crowd and sent people a-scatter. But two of the officers were dragged from their horses and attacked, each sustaining injuries, and all were recalled to the police station. One of the horses sustained cuts.

At 11 o'clock a magistrate, Mr W.T. Coles, arrived and read out the Riot Act. Almost certainly hardly anyone would have heard him in the commotion, but the law required its reading. It did no good. Soon every window of the shop premises of Messrs Fisher and Longley was shattered, and with the barricades of the latter's shop now torn down the mob entered and began throwing the contents into the street. Calico, chintz and other materials were passed about in the

---

The Riot Act

A riot was 'an unlawful assembly of three or more persons which had begun to execute the purpose for which it assembled by a breach of the peace and to the terror of the public'. The lawful proclamation read out to the mob by the magistrate was as follows:

"Our Sovereign Lord the King chargeth and commandeth all persons being assembled immediately to disperse themselves and peaceably depart to their habitations or to their lawful business upon the pains contained in the Act made in the first year of King George for preventing tumultuous and riotous assemblies. God save the King!"

To obstruct the reading of the proclamation was a felony, punishable with penal servitude for life.

The Act required the justices to seize and apprehend all persons continuing after one hour and indemnified them and those who acted under their authority from liabilities from injuries caused thereby.

---

crowd 'with shouts of drunken glee', and one of the mob was reported waving a gay-coloured parasol over his head. Women and children were seen darting through the crowd, carrying bundles of drapery partly concealed under their clothing. The police formed a cordon, whereupon the mob turned their attention to another shop belonging to Mr Longley.

This shop sold boots and shoes. Stones shattered the windows as the mob entered and stole contents. The crowd now surged back to the shop of Mr Fisher. He, too, had tried to barricade his premises, but the crowd used clothes props, staves and metal pipes to force their way inside. Mr Fisher and his sons stoutly tried to defend their property, and as the mob entered they brought down the metal shutters on the hands of the assailants, an act which sparked off the rumour, later reported in the London newspapers, that Mr Fisher and his men were using meat cleavers to chop off people's fingers. Injuries to assailants' hands and other body parts would later be useful to help police identify them. One wonders how Mr Fisher and his sons would have stood if events had taken place today, on the issue of 'reasonable force'. Did they exceed their powers in defending their property? In any event, when the crowd got inside they tried to set the shop on fire, piling up furniture and using paper and spirits collected from Mr Longley's drapery shop. The fire brigade was called, but even as they were putting out the fire there were attempts to cut their hoses. It seems that, whilst Mr Fisher and his family fought hard to defend their property, Mr Longley stood back and accepted that although he could not prevent the inevitable, he was able to look at the faces of the mob, so that he could later identify the guilty.

By this time many windows of other shops in the Market Place had been shattered, but then police strength increased with the return of officers from Hemel Hempstead and another batch of 20 from the Metropolitan Police who had travelled up from Euston. They had about 40 men. It wasn't enough.

Superintendent Wood was the senior police officer. With the Riot Act read, he appealed for special constables to help regular officers contain the mob. Astonishingly, five hundred men came forward. Two hundred were sworn in. They were issued with truncheons and sticks. Squads were formed, each under the command of a regular, uniformed officer, and these charged the crowds, wielding batons and rounding up ringleaders. One can imagine the scene: baton-wielding specials sorting out the mob, personal battles here and there on Watford's great night of shame.

There were injuries all round, to policemen and rioters alike, none serious, which in the circumstances was astonishing. By 3 a.m. the police had control of the town, and later, assisted by the specials and council 'scavenging staff', they began a clean-up operation of streets of broken glass and stones, pieces of wood and pools of blood (much as they do today in Watford on Saturday mornings). As for the cost of the damage, under the law the town would have to pay. Those whose property had suffered by riot had the civil remedy of bringing an action against the Cassio Hundred, where the riot occurred. This was a pre-Norman Conquest obligation, still valid then, based on the premise that the 'Hundred' was supposed to preserve law and order, which it had failed to do after the Riot Act had been read, even though it had not been possible. The charges, when they were brought, would not be under the Act, but in respect of damage, larceny (theft) and assault.

That Friday morning, Chief Constable Henry Daniell, arrived at Watford, along with Deputy Chief Constable John Reynolds. Arrangements were made to deal with any further disturbances, of which there were none, save a few sporadic incidents. This left the police with the task of arresting offenders, along with the recovery of stolen property.

John Reynolds had a reputation as a good copper. In fact, he served the Constabulary for 51 years before retirement. He it was who over thirty years previously had arrested John Chapman for the murder of PC Benjamin Snow at Benington, and he it was who now organised the arrests of ringleaders and others, most of whom were knocked from their beds the morning after the night before. He, indeed everyone, knew the police had not far to look for the guilty: the slums of Ballard's Buildings, Red Lion Yard and their environs. The *Watford Observer* contrived to create a typical arrest: 'A knock at the door. Sleeping rioter: "Who's there?" Constable: "Police." Rioter: "What's up?" Constable: "You know what's up." Rioter: "I've been in bed since half past six." Unbelieving Constable: "Come along." Rioter: "Well, I suppose I'll have to go through it." '

By 10 a.m. there were 35 prisoners, including eight women, in the cells, all described as rough looking and crestfallen, as well as cut and bruised. They were brought before the magistrates, and with the Chief Constable — 'in his neat riding breeches' — and DCC Reynolds present at court, all were remanded in custody to St Albans prison. They were taken to St Albans on the 11.38 a.m. train. A large crowd watched them go. The crowd expressed much sympathy for Messrs Fisher and Longley, and disgust at the disgrace the rioters had brought upon

Watford. Mr Fisher said that although there had been no meat in his shop at the time of the attack, two pairs of scales had been damaged, as well as extensive damage to the shop premises. A large butcher's knife had been taken and had been recovered in a nearby garden. He knew he would receive compensation, which amounted to between £80 and £100. Business continued in Mr Longley's shops, despite the damage. He estimated his loss, including stolen goods, at £1,000.

The following Tuesday the prisoners were brought from St Albans to the Magistrates' Court at Watford in a police van, a bus and a waggonette. Mounted police formed an escort as the crowds turned out to watch them pass. There was no trouble. The prisoners, now numbering 54, were placed in the cells. Before proceedings began, the Chairman thanked the 500 who had volunteered their services as special constables, and remarked, 'We must all regret that the violence of the mob was directed to the property of two gentlemen who have consistently shown liberality and great feeling for those less fortunately placed.' He praised the police, including Supt Wood, then proceedings began with prosecution counsel offering comment on the riot, the reading of the Riot Act, the injuries to police officers, including to Inspector Boutell who had a cut head, and the arrests and recovery of stolen property. Some, not all, of the cases are included here...

The first concerned one of identification, not surprisingly a major issue in a riot situation. It concerned Frederick Penny, of Fearnley Street. Sergeant Peck said he saw Penny inside Mr Longley's shop with articles of clothing in his hand, which he threw down on sight of the officer, and ran away. Sgt Peck caught him, 'without losing sight of him', and arrested him. Penny denied this, saying he was with a friend named Doggett. The case had to be adjourned until his friend attended, which he did. Doggett said he was with Penny from 8 o'clock until he was arrested, and that they both remained outside the shop. He said Sgt Peck came from the churchyard and saw a number of people running and arrested Penny. The court took into

Procession of the accused
Prisoners being taken to King's Street police station, Watford
From 'The Book of Watford', by J.B. Nunn
Reproduced with kind permission of Mrs Linda Nunn

consideration his good character and sentenced him to one month's imprisonment.

Frank Walters was next. He was arrested by Sgt Peck at home. The prisoner's wife was present. She produced five new pairs of boots and a piece of chintz. Walters said he picked them up and said there was nothing else, but the police found more boots under a chair. They belonged to Mr Longley. Walters was convicted, but sentence was postponed. Sergeant Dolley said he went to a house at Red Lion Yard where he found twelve new aprons hidden among linen. He arrested Elizabeth Bransford, who had hidden the stolen property. She was Fined £2. Harvey Hedge of Water Lane was charged with stealing 16 boots. Constable Wright went to his house where he saw his wife, who said there were no boots in the house. The officer went inside and found them on a couch. Hedge said he'd found them and was going to take them back. He was fined £2. Alice Freeman and Henrietta Brown were arrested by Constable Steel, who saw them gathering boots that had been thrown out of the shop of Mr Longley. Each woman was sentenced to one month's hard labour.

Alfred Arthur Lodge of Ballard's Buildings was described as a ringleader. Constable Pitcher said he saw him throwing stones at windows. Constable Epithite saw him breaking windows with a piece of wood, and Constable Davies saw him throwing bundles from a window. He was sentenced to two months' hard labour. William Cain was charged with wilful damage. A witness for the defence said he saw Cain being 'knocked about' in the churchyard by the police. Cain was given one month's hard labour. Thomas Hawes of Ballard's Buildings was charged with wilful damage and dragging goods from Mr Longley's shop. 'I never done nothing,' said Hawes. Elizabeth Robson, who lived with him, said he went to bed till 12 o'clock, went out and then stayed in. Hawes was given six weeks' hard labour.

Ezekiel Franklin of Ballard's Buildings was charged with wilful damage – throwing stones at shops. He had five previous convictions and was given six weeks' hard labour. Victoria Wilson was charged with wilful damage. She had emerged from Ballard's Buildings with a clothes prop and allegedly broke a window in Mr Fisher's shop. No-one had actually seen her do it. She denied doing any damage. She was sentenced to one month's hard labour. William George Birch of Ballard's Buildings was charged with wilful damage. He was seen carrying a hatful of stones and distributing them, and throwing some himself. Fined £2.

And so it went on, each case following the one before, many prisoners pleading not guilty. There were cases where the evidence, especially of identification, seemed sparse. But the damage had been done, the property had been stolen, and much of it recovered and they were the ones in the dock. It was as well for them that no-one was charged under the Riot Act, charges which would have carried sentences of penal servitude. Whether justice was done in all cases one might wonder. The cost to the town under the terms of the Riot Act was over £2,000. The cost to Watford's good name was immeasurable.

As the prisoners sentenced to imprisonment were taken through the streets, many displayed bravado; but it was noted that as the last houses were passed and they were no longer in view of the crowd, their faces changed and some were seen to be in tears. King Edward made a full recovery and was crowned on 9th August, when the rearranged Watford Coronation festivities took place. Thousands passed through the gates of Cassiobury Park and a great day was had by all.

The Verdict

There can be no condoning a riot, no matter how just the rioters' cause. Riots lead to other crimes, just as they did at Watford: damage and assault, theft and receiving stolen property, not to mention the fear and apprehension placed in the minds of law abiding citizens. The guilty deserved to be punished, though let it be said there seems room for doubt that all who were apprehended were guilty as charged.

And all the while Mr Fisher and his council colleagues, prosperous all, seemed not to care much if at all about the squalor in their town. Many of them would have attended St Mary's Church on Sundays. Did they worship God and emerge to face the slums, just yards away, with consciences clear and an 'it's got nothing to do with us' attitude? Could they not have done something to alleviate the living conditions the rioters had to endure? There but for fortune, indeed. The rioters stand condemned; so, in a sense, does Watford's council.

Ballard's Buildings

"Hot-foot from slumdom"

The rioters punished, the Coronation festivities duly celebrated, whom can we blame for Watford's day of shame? The King? Hardly. He was ill with a life-threatening condition requiring immediate surgery; it wasn't his fault. Mr Francis Fisher and the town council? Their decision, to cancel festivities, was reasonable in the circumstances. Those who would riot, cause damage and strike fear into law-abiding citizens? Certainly.

Consider, though, how disappointed those lowly men and women must have been, those slum dwellers who would have looked forward to a day of celebration and gay festivity, an occasion to lighten their miserable lives. Take heed of the *Watford Critic*, a monthly journal published in the town, 'a democratic chronicle of Town happenings', as it described itself. 'Mr Francis Fisher's chickens have come home to roost', wrote the Critic. 'The precise spirit of rowdyism which he has done as much as anyone in the town to arouse, and which expressed itself in the bacchanalian junketing of celebration day, culminated in the sack of business premises, including those of Mr Fisher himself'.

The Critic deplored the scenes as much as anyone, but out of evil good had come. 'A scrutiny of the addresses of the persons dealt with by the Bench for rioting and looting should provide much reflection. By far the greatest percentage (of rioters) came hot-foot from slumdom.' Ballard's Buildings alone produced eleven hooligans, Red Lion Yard, Tipple's Yard and Meeting Alley three each. 'We would not assert that ill-housing alone is responsible for ruffianism, but that the low moral atmosphere generated in stifling and pestiferous court and alley is an important factor. The Coronation Committee stand condemned. They promoted arrangements, not only for the festive entertainment of the needy, but also to provide schoolchildren with money, which it was feared would find its way into parents' pockets. Accustomed to closing their eyes to the existence of the slums, the Committee blundered with consummate blindness. They have now learned to recognise slumdom as a nursery of vice, a factor in the degrading outbursts of rowdyism which all sane men deplore'. Strong words.

The Critic was putting the blame for housing conditions on the council: conditions suffered by people without means, without today's state benefits, without dignity, without anything compared to the Francis Fishers of the world. Ballard's Buildings were a row of 17th-century cottages, and afterwards, where other old buildings were demolished, they somehow survived, situated where the public toilets now stand at Church Street multi-storey car park. Here were overflowing cesspits, open dungholes, blocked sewers and drains with sewage seeping through walls from one dwelling into the next, where people kept pigs and slaughterhouses next door to housing, some 225 in all – probably more, truth be known, 'incomers' from London, the Midlands and the North, and Ireland. A report concluded: 'They (residents) have no means of disposing of refuse matter, liquid or solid, except by throwing it into open cesspools, or into the surface drains which lead into the open side channels in the main street'.

From here, and similar homes, came the Coronation Day rioters. Is it any wonder they were so disappointed at the cancellation of a party? Had Mr Fisher and his Committee, and the good citizens of Watford for that matter, any right to be surprised by their conduct? Ballard's Buildings were demolished in 1926. You might care to reflect on its occupants and the wretched conditions in which they lived next time you stroll through Millennium Square.

4

RICKMANSWORTH 1911

"With very great brutality"

The Charles Coleman Case

That Charles Coleman had been with Rose Anna Gurney on the night in question was not in doubt: they had drank together in the King's Head at Watford, and gone on, by train, to the Swan Hotel, Rickmansworth. Later, about ten past ten, Henry Ginger, night watchman at Salter's Brewery, who knew Polly, as Rose was sometimes known, had seen her walking with a man he thought was the accused who, he said, had called out 'Goodnight, Ginger' to him before the couple passed through the railway arch towards a stile that led into Rickmansworth Park. They were in shadow, so he did not see whether they actually entered the park. There was no-one else about, he said. They did not go as far as the Catholic church, he was certain.

At 8 o'clock the next morning, Rose's body was found in the park by Katherine Atley and her sister, of Chorleywood, on their way to church. 'She was murdered under circumstances of very great brutality,' said Mr Mathew for the prosecution, at the trial of Charles Coleman. Her body had been 'shockingly mutilated', with at least nineteen stab wounds. The man seen with her the previous evening had to be prime suspect, but was it Charles Coleman? No, said Coleman, who said he and Rose had 'met two chaps' at the railway arch, one of whom she had called George. 'Wait a minute Charlie,' she had said to Coleman, who replied, 'I'm off, it's no use me waiting here for you.' He had left her then, he said. No-one had seen him enter the park with Rose, and there was no direct evidence to connect him to the crime. So the prosecution, seeking to show the jury the kind of man Charles Coleman was, would tell them of his past record instead. 'Would you like to read his convictions?' asked Mr Mathew. Superintendent Wood obliged.

Coleman, the court heard, had been convicted for breaking and entering houses, indecent behaviour in a church, larceny, wilful damage, game trespass and assault. On one occasion he had been charged with attempted murder: 'In 1897,' said Supt Wood, 'he was lodging in a cottage, and when the landlord got up one morning to go to work he (Coleman) went to the landlady's room and cut her throat with a razor. She had to jump out of the window to get away from him.' Coleman was convicted of wounding her. 'Before that, he was convicted of stealing a watch, being drunk and disorderly, stealing a fowl, and trying to commit suicide (a criminal offence then) by hanging himself in the police station.' He added that Coleman had also been convicted of mutilating a dog. 'Do you know whether the prisoner has ever suffered from sunstroke?' he was asked. 'I do not,' replied Supt Wood.

Hearing this, any doubts the jury may have harnessed about whether Charles Coleman had killed Rose Anna Gurney would surely have been dispelled. There remained one other issue, the question of his 'sanity'. Was it murder or manslaughter? It was vital. Charles Coleman's life depended upon it.

Rose Gurney lived in Church Lane, Mill End. She was seen at home on the day in question day by her daughter, Eleanor, at 4.30 p.m., after which Rose said she was off to Watford to buy some clothes. Mary Ann Peek, a neighbour, saw Coleman and Rose drinking together in the Swan Hotel, Rickmansworth, about 9.40 p.m., apparently on friendly terms. When he testified at the inquest, Henry Ginger, the

The King's Head, Watford
Scene of a drinking session by Charles Coleman and Rose Gurney
From 'The Book of Watford', by J.B. Nunn
Reproduced with kind permission of Mrs Linda Nunn

night watchman, was unable to positively confirm the identity of the man who Rose Anna was with when they passed him near the railway arch; at the trial in November, however, he said he was sure it was Coleman.

Charles Coleman was 36, Rose was a widow, about 50 years of age. The discovery of her body at eight o'clock that Sunday morning, about ninety yards from the stile over which she and her attacker would probably have crossed, must have been a harrowing experience. She was found lying on her back, with two pools of blood nearby. Her blouse and skirt were 'saturated with blood', and two parcels lay some yards away – possibly the clothing she said she would buy in Watford. A piece of a blood-stained newspaper lay about ten yards away.

Dr Clarke had been called to the scene. Death had occurred between eight and ten hours previously, he said. Some of the stab

The Cock public house, Church End, Sarratt
Scene of the arrest of Charles Coleman

wounds could not have been self inflicted. Two of the upper wounds to the chest had punctured a lung and the heart. Many of the wounds were superficial, three 'serious'. She also had defensive wounds to her hands. There were stab-wounds to her buttocks and her back, in his opinion caused after death. He was asked if he thought Rose's assailant 'might have been a madman'. 'He might or he might not,' said Dr Clarke.

It wasn't long before the police had identified their suspect. At one o'clock the next day Police Constable Clark went to the Cock public house, Church End, Sarratt, where he found Charles Coleman drinking from a bottle of beer. The constable searched him and found a pocket knife. When told he was being arrested for murder, Coleman, replied, 'What shall you want me for next? If I had known you were coming I would have put my head under a train. I admit I was with her, but I left her against the Brewery about 10.30 p.m.

talking to two men. I don't know who they were. It was dark.' On the way to Rickmansworth police station he declared, 'I hope they will hang me.' When asked by defence counsel if he had seen anything in Coleman's demeanour to show he was not sane, PC Clark said he was aware he had been convicted for mutilating a dog.

Superintendent Wood said that there was blood on the sleeve of Coleman's jacket. Coleman said he didn't think it was blood. In those days, it would be difficult if not impossible to prove the blood, if it was, was that of Rose Anna Gurney, or even whether it was human. The piece of newspaper may have borne the murderer's fingerprints; sadly, such identification methods were not available to the police then.

Dr William Willcox was senior scientific analyst at the Home Office. He examined Coleman's pocket knife and clothing. There was no blood on the knife, but it could easily have been wiped or washed off. He formed the opinion that the blood found on the sleeve of his jacket, and some on his shirt, had been 'treated with water'. A special effort had been made to remove the bloodstain from the shirt. In his opinion the blood was 'mammalian'. There were also signs of blood on Coleman's waistcoat. He said one of the stains on the piece of newspaper showed a 'straight line', as though an object had been wiped on it. All bloodstains were fairly recent.

Had the prosecution proved beyond reasonable doubt that Charles Coleman had killed Rose Anna Gurney, and, if so, was he sane enough to be responsible for his actions?

The evidence of Henry Ginger, the night watchman, was crucial. At the inquest, just days after the crime, he had not been certain about the identity of the man with Rose; four months later he was able to tell a jury he was. Coleman said two men had appeared and he had left Rose near the railway arch. Whether or not the jury thought Coleman was the killer, they would first hear evidence about his sanity or otherwise. The first to testify in this regard was Dr Charles Parker, formerly of Rickmansworth, now of Wimpole Street, London.

Dr Parker had examined Coleman, and had given evidence at his trial for attempted murder, in 1897. His opinion then had been that Coleman was not 'mentally responsible', and that he was likely to have 'fits of passion'. His illness, he said, was nameless. 'There are people who are not quite mentally sound who are liable to do things that those who are quite unsound would not do'. Whether the jury, or indeed anyone, was able to comprehend the meaning of this remark is not clear, but the Judge, probably seeking a reply in the King's English, asked him, 'You mean he is not in sound mental condition... the fact of a commission of a crime is evidence of insanity?' Dr Parker said the mutilation of the dog showed an unbalanced mind. He agreed his evidence was of his recollection of Coleman's condition 14 years ago. Superintendent Wood gave details about the mutilation of the dog, but these were not reported upon, the Georgian press being reticent in such matters.

Members of the Coleman family stepped forward to testify on his behalf. John Coleman told the court his brother Charles had found his (John's) son drowning 15 years before and had 'never seemed the same man since'. Then eight years ago Charles had had an accident at Harefield Asbestos Works, when he was pulled round by a belt and sustained a broken arm, as well as injuries to his leg and 'his insides'. He said Charles had tried to commit suicide at Rickmansworth Park the previous January, and had woken up the following morning with a rope around his neck. A few glasses of drink would 'upset' him, he said. Another brother, George Coleman, said he once 'fetched' Charles out of the water at Mill End. Charles had said, 'I was after a man,' yet there had been no-one there. Emma Austin, Coleman's sister, said Charles had tried to commit suicide at her home, and had threatened to do so on two or three other occasions. She had sometimes detained him to thwart suicide attempts, and her son had held Coleman down when he said he would cut his own throat. Elizabeth Clark, another sister, said that about a month before the cruelty to a dog incident Coleman had said, 'Oh my poor head. I think I shall go mad,' and six months before that he had declared, 'Oh dear, what shall I do, my head does feel funny.'

Dr Dyer, Medical Officer of H.M. Prison, Brixton, said Coleman had been under his supervision whilst on remand. He said Coleman 'was a degenerate type, but had no delusions, no hallucinations and he could find no evidence of insanity'. Coleman, he said, was rather morose and depraved, but otherwise perfectly rational. Mr Taylor, defence barrister, said that Coleman's whole career showed there was 'something more than sheer criminality in the prisoner'. He had a diseased mind. No man would mutilate a dog as he had if he was in his right mind.

The Judge pointed out that if the jury found Coleman guilty (of killing Rose) they had to consider his state of mind. A man was responsible for his actions if he knew the difference between right and wrong. Did Coleman know he had done wrong? With regard to the evidence of his brothers and sisters, the curious part was that no application was ever made to 'lock this man up and take charge of him'. The questions left to the jury were: was Coleman the man who took the life of this woman; and, if he was, was there something in this case to show he was mentally deficient and not responsible for his actions? The jury took seven minutes to find Coleman guilty of murder. They had decided he was of sound mind.

The Judge addressed Charles Coleman. 'After a careful and patient hearing of your case, the jury have come to the only conclusion possible. For what reason you did this no-one can tell, but that you did it there is no doubt. You knew perfectly well what you were doing. Your whole history shows a career of crime. There has not been the slightest suggestion you were not responsible for your actions, except in 1897, for the purpose of getting you off a serious matter.' He sentenced him to be 'hung by the neck until you are dead, your body to be then buried within the precincts of the prison'. Coleman, smiling throughout, said, 'I am very pleased to hear it. May I see my friends?' 'Certainly,' said the Judge. Sound mind indeed.

The Verdict

D id Charles Coleman kill Rose Anna Gurney? No motive was established; there was no suggestion or apparent evidence of sexual assault; Coleman made no admission, not even when facing death on the scaffold when he had nothing to lose. He had a knife. So did lots of others. His clothing had been washed in areas apparently bloodstained. He had been seen with Rose. He had previous convictions for violence.

A h yes, previous convictions. All made known to the jury *before* they retired to consider their verdict. What a terrible record. Of course he killed Rose. As to *mens rea*, his criminal intent: Counsel for the defence would have known all along of the likelihood that the jury would conclude that Charles Coleman had killed Rose Anna Gurney. Their objective would, therefore, be to convince them that Coleman, if not actually insane, was nonetheless short of a full shilling. The prosecution, anticipating this, sought to prove otherwise. Asking a policeman if he knew whether the accused had ever suffered from sunstroke may seem trite, even amusing, but the superintendent's reply, that he had not, suited their purpose. As did the testimony of Dr Dyer, who said he could find 'no evidence of insanity'. Even the Judge shared the prosecution's view. Summing up, he said, 'The jury have come to the only conclusion possible... You knew perfectly well what you were doing.'

D r Parker, who had examined Coleman 14 years before, said that his opinion then had been that Coleman was not 'mentally responsible'. (One wonders why an up to date medical report of Coleman's mental condition was not prepared). Then there is the combined testimony of Coleman's brothers and sisters: several suicide attempts, talks of suicide, odd behaviour by brother Charles. The Judge commented, 'The curious part was that no application was ever made to 'lock this man up and take charge of him.' It seems the responsibility to have someone taken into care on account of mental illness was that of the family, not a doctor. So, by not having Charles certified his family mustn't have considered him insane or mentally ill.

I n fact, Charles Coleman probably did kill Rose. And if we cannot find a motive it is probably because he was drunk. He and Rose had been drinking all evening, first at Watford, then at Rickmansworth. They were probably seen together close to the time they would have entered the park. Then – who knows? Maybe they had an argument and alcohol, that ingredient in so many violent crimes, took a hand. He had a knife; he used it in a frenzied attack, stabbing her again and again while she put up her hands in futile attempts to stop him. It was brutal and merciless. Today Charles Coleman would probably be convicted of manslaughter on the grounds of diminished responsibility, an option not open to the jury at that time.

The Execution of Charles Coleman

Charles Coleman was hanged at St Albans prison on Thursday, 21st December, 1911, 'a dull, cheerless morning with a drizzling rain prevailing...'

It seems his imminent execution was scarcely known to the residents of St Albans. Nevertheless, a considerable crowd gathered, thanks to the execution notice, pinned to the prison gate the night before, which stated: 'The sentence of the law passed upon Charles Coleman, found guilty of murder, will be carried into execution at 8 a.m. tomorrow'. Passers-by, many bound for their trains into London, lingered, looking for the hoisting of the black flag which would signify when the execution had taken place.

Coleman never confessed to the crime, saying, 'Well, if I did it, I did it, but I don't remember anything about it.' He showed little concern about his fate, only requesting 'a smoke', which was granted. The executioner was John Ellis, who entered his cell a minute before 8 o'clock, pinioned him and led him across the prison yard to the execution shed just behind the prison gate. Coleman remained calm. Once on the scaffold, Ellis placed the white cap over his head and asked him, 'Are you ready?' It is doubtful that he awaited an answer as he pulled the lever and Coleman dropped through the trapdoor.

As to the black flag, the crowd waited in vain, as the practice of hoisting it had been abandoned. As they watched, puzzled by its non-appearance, the prison door opened and the Reverend Robinson, the chaplain, emerged and cycled off, followed by Dr Lipcombe, the prison surgeon, who 'left in his motor'. No doubt the crowd then drew its own conclusions.

Waltham Cross 1914

The Last Execution

Everything went wrong for George Anderson the day his wife died. They had lived for two years at the same address as Joseph Whybrow and his wife, Harriett, a mid-terraced house in Waltham Cross. Harriett was Anderson's stepdaughter. The two couples had got along fine, it seems. Both men were in employment, Anderson as a labourer, and Joseph Whybrow worked at the Royal Gunpowder factory at Waltham Abbey.

Anderson's wife died on 9th June, 1914. Thereafter, he gave up going to work and remained at home instead. One can sympathise with his loss, but not with the manner in which he decided to deal with it – getting drunk. This was all very well, but Joseph Whybrow would be at work whilst his young wife, Harriett, 31, was left alone in the house with 59-year-old Anderson. It proved to be a recipe for disaster, ending up with her callous murder, on the street, in broad daylight.

Emma Whitbread lived next door. From her house (if she was looking) she could see through the open back door of the Whybrows', and even beyond into the scullery and parlour. She could hear what was going on, too. Which was, she told the Hertfordshire Assizes at Anderson's trial, 'friendly relations' taking place between Anderson and his step-daughter. Just after eleven o'clock on Saturday, 27th June, for example, after Whybrow had left to go to work, Mrs Whitbread saw Harriett sitting on Anderson's lap. When Whybrow returned home early that day, there followed a 'disturbance' between him and Anderson. Just after five o'clock, when Mrs Whitbread saw Whybrow and Harriett in the kitchen, Anderson appeared. She told the court, 'He snatched up a chair and got possession of a chopper and said, "I will kill the pair of you".' The police were called, but

Anderson quietened down before they arrived. That night he slept in an outhouse.

On Monday Anderson apologised to Whybrow for the disturbance. Whybrow said he would not allow him to stay in the house, after which he went to work. Later, Mrs Whitbread saw Harriett sitting on Anderson's lap again. The following day Whybrow went to work as usual, and about 10 a.m. Mrs Whitbread saw Anderson and Harriett drinking beer from the same glass. At one o'clock she heard them 'quarrelling and scuffling'. She could hear 'perfectly well' what was going on. 'The walls are so thin,' she said. When she hurried outside, she saw Anderson holding Harriett by the neck. 'Whatever are you doing?' she asked. 'My life is a fair misery,' he replied. Later, when Harriett went out, Mrs Whitbread heard Anderson sharpening a knife, saying to himself, 'That will do nicely.'

Shortly afterwards, Harriett and Anderson were seen having an argument in Eleanor Cross Road by Philip Henry Rodwell, a lad who sold bananas. As he told the jury, 'I saw the prisoner put his right hand into his right-hand pocket and pull out a knife, open it behind him and draw it across her throat.' Then he saw Anderson calmly fold the knife and walk into a nearby pub. Charlotte Hicks, who lived nearby, heard Harriett's screams. 'You have cut my throat, now you are satisfied.' Harriett collapsed and was laid in a nearby garden by Mrs Hicks who tried to stop the blood-flow. She died before medical help arrived, her jugular vein severed.

Young Rodwell found a policeman, PC Darlington of Cheshunt. The constable went to the pub, took possession of the knife and arrested Anderson, who said, 'She has been aggravating me for some time. I don't care if I hang.' He testified at his trial anyway, his defence being that he and Harriett had argued, that she had told him to go to hell and knocked his tobacco tin from his hand. As he turned to leave her, she caught hold of his coat sleeve. He threw his arm around her and his hand 'got alongside of her neck.' When asked why he did not help Harriett, now on the ground with her throat cut, he replied, 'I

St Albans Prison
Venue of Hertfordshire's last execution
Photo: The Watford Observer

did not think it was so bad.' There followed detailed questioning, including by the judge, as to how it was possible to cut someone's throat accidentally. 'It was as I turned round,' said Anderson.

Mr Bernard, defending, said he was sure the jury would pay as much care and attention to the case of this 'poor broken down, drink-sodden creature' as they would if Anderson was a man endowed with quality that inspired respect. If he had wanted to kill Harriett, he could have done so in the house. There were none of the features of a planned and deliberate murder. The jury took 17 minutes to disagree. 'The sentence of the law,' the Judge told Anderson, 'is that you be taken from this place to a place of execution and that you be hanged by the neck until you are dead. May the Lord have mercy on your soul.'

George Anderson was hanged at St Albans prison at eight o'clock on 23rd December, 1914. The executioner, as in the Coleman case, was John Ellis, 'a competent and experienced man'. It was Hertfordshire's last execution. No-one waited at the prison gates that fateful hour, although the prison would become famous enough in later years as the place of incarceration of the fictitious Norman Stanley Fletcher, in *Porridge*. As for John Ellis, he spent 23 years of his life hanging people in the name of justice. Eighteen years after he hanged George Anderson for cutting his victim's throat, he took his own life when he cut his throat with a razor.

5

Bricket Wood 1917

The Shooting of Janet Oven

At 5 a.m. on Friday, 18th May, 1917, as John Knight Oven was preparing to leave home to go to work at Leavesden Asylum, near Watford, he noticed that his daughter, Janet, was asleep in her bed. He saw her head and shoulders as he passed the bedroom door. He could not have known that the next time he would see her would be later that same day in St Albans mortuary, where Janet had been taken after being shot twice at close range on a country lane, murdered by person or persons unknown.

Janet Oven was 26, and described as 'jolly-looking, intelligent and hard-working'. She had been walking along Mount Pleasant Lane, Bricket Wood, towards the railway station to catch the 8.42 train to Watford, where she worked as a saleswoman and buyer for Mr James Cawdell at his draper's shop in Watford High Street. She had only lived with her parents and two sisters at their rented home at Waterdell Farm Cottages, Garston, since March. Before that she had lived in Hull, where she had worked for six years, before returning to her parents.

Janet had left the house at 8.30 a.m. Her route would have taken her along a road now occupied by Junction 6 of the M1 motorway, and thence along Mount Pleasant Lane, in those days a quiet country byway. She had been seen passing by a Mrs Jordan, who lived in a cottage. Janet was reading a book as she walked, and carried a cardboard case containing her work clothing, a dress.

Miss Janet Oven
The Herts Advertiser & St Albans Times

Shortly after Janet passed their house on Mount Pleasant Lane, Norman Thain Davidson, a London solicitor, and his wife, Joyce, left their residence, The White House, also to walk to the railway station. As they left the drive of their property Mrs Davidson heard a shot. Immediately after they saw a man some 200 or 300 yards ahead run across the road, where he disappeared into the woods on the left. When they reached the spot where he had disappeared they saw Janet's cardboard case and a little further on her book, both lying in the road, and further on again they saw a small pool of blood. Then, on the right, by a grassy bank about the spot where today a street known as West Riding adjoins Mount Pleasant Lane, they saw Janet lying in a shallow ditch, dead, her umbrella cord still around her wrist. Ironically, the book she had been reading, 'The Purloined Prince', had a picture of a man pointing a gun on the front cover.

Mount Pleasant Lane, Bricket Wood

Another resident, Susan Powell, heard two shots being fired. She thought it was someone shooting rabbits, a not unusual occurrence. Earlier, Mrs Powell had seen Janet's two sisters pass along the lane, followed by Janet a quarter of an hour later, then the shots. She confirmed that Janet had been reading as she walked, and that she was alone. She also said that she had seen a strange man, not that morning, but on several other occasions before. He was always alone.

Meanwhile, Mr Davidson returned home and called the police. The Deputy Chief Constable, Mr Wood, attended within quarter of an hour from Watford. He found a large pool of blood by the side of the road, and saw that Janet was lying face down in the ditch and that she had been shot in the head and in the neck. Her clothing was not disturbed and there was no sign of a struggle. It seemed she would have died instantly.

Some three hours later, the police surgeon, Leslie Bates, attended the scene. His opinion was that after being shot Janet had been dragged from the road to the ditch. Her body was taken to St Albans mortuary, where examination showed a bullet wound to the temple surrounded by numerous particles of gunpowder driven into the skin by the closeness of the shot. Opposite the wound was a comminuted fracture of the skull. A piece of bone from the skull had become detached, and on it he found a bullet. An inch and a quarter below the lobe of the left ear was another, similar bullet wound. This bullet had narrowly missed the spinal cord and caused no apparent serious injury. This bullet was not found.

Theories abounded. Perhaps Janet had been shot by stray bullets from a poacher's gun. But two stray shots seemed unlikely, especially when the bullet recovered by Mr Bates proved to have been discharged from a pistol. Perhaps the second shot, heard by Mrs Powell, might have been the murderer committing suicide. But the lack of another body nearby scotched this theory. Maybe the killer was someone Janet knew, from Hull perhaps, someone who had had a secret relationship with her. It seemed the answer might lie with the torn fragments of a letter found nearby, from a secret lover, maybe. Alas, this proved to be unconnected. Janet Oven had been shot dead at close range, evidently by a stranger, and dumped in a ditch. But why?

Robbery seemed the most likely motive. Although Janet's purse was still in her pocket, it was established that her handbag, containing a few coppers, some dress material and a few letters, was missing. Mr Wood enlisted the help of over 100 special constables as well as regular officers, to search the extensive woodland near the scene for traces of Janet's property or any other clues. Enquiries were made at railway stations but these yielded nothing. Had the murderer escaped on foot, by car or even on a bicycle? No-one could say. Meanwhile the police released the description of the man seen by Mr and Mrs Davidson and Mrs Powell. He was described as about 30 years, 5 ft 8 in tall, wearing a dark brown overcoat, grey loose trousers and a cloth cap. He was clean shaven and respectable looking. Mrs Jordan

TRAGEDY AT BRICKET WOOD.

YOUNG WOMAN FATALLY SHOT.

POLICE SCOUR THE DISTRICT FOR UNKNOWN MAN.

INQUEST PROCEEDINGS.

As briefly announced in our last issue, a young woman, named Janet Oven, aged 26 and single, the daughter of an attendant at the Leavesden Asylum, was shot last Friday morning whilst on her way to catch the morning train for Watford, where she was employed by Mr. Cawdell, draper, and for a week past the greatest sensation has been aroused in the district as a consequence. A "Herts Advertiser" representative was the first on the spot, and in his interview with the distressed mother and daughter, and added that she had seen this man several times during last week, dawdling along as if thinking hard about something. The local postman also saw him on Friday morning. A fresh sensation was caused by the discovery of the fragments of a letter, written on a ruled sheet torn from a writing pad, which were found near the spot, and by a strange coincidence the book which was picked up, and which presumably the victim had been carrying, bore the title of "The Purloined Prince," with an illustration on the front cover of a man in the act of aiming a revolver

"Tragedy at Bricket Wood"

The Herts Advertiser & St Albans Times, 26 May 1917

remarked that it had occurred to her that such a man ought to be in the army, like her own son. There were plenty of young men in the army just then, dying in the fields of France and Belgium.

The search of the woods was seen as vital, and 300–400 specials from around the county were deployed to search again areas searched the week before. The police were desperate to find something to provide just a whiff of a clue. It was even reported that aeroplanes were circling above the woods — not at the behest of the police, let it be said — although what anyone could hope to see from above is anyone's guess. On the ground the police had their reward when an overcoat and cap were discovered, the former of such smart appearance that a sergeant was heard to describe it as 'a very decent garment, one which I would not be ashamed to wear myself,' thus supporting the 'respectable looking' description of the strange man seen near the scene of the crime. But their discovery led the police nowhere. Indeed, the only reasonable conclusion they could draw from the scant evidence they had was that a strange man had been seen hanging around for several days and would therefore have probably known that Janet Oven would pass by that morning at the relevant time. Whether or not he knew her was unknown, but police enquiries, including in Hull, had proved negative in this regard. There was no known man in Janet's life. If there had been, then there could be some premeditated reason for her murder; if not, the motive for the crime was probably the theft of her handbag and other property, however trivial, unless Janet's killer was a madman. It was a tough one for the police to crack. As the *Watford Observer* reported, 'If Deputy Chief Constable Wood and his staff track down the dastardly author of the outrage at Bricket Wood, it will infinitely be to their credit'. Quite so, but the following July, when the same newspaper reported that a youth had been charged with the murder, it was not down to the work of the police, it was down to the killer admitting it of his own volition.

Janet's killer was a 16-year-old youth called Albert Edward Lorford whose conscience, it seems, had driven him to confession. Indeed, he all but confessed to a former school chum called Mures, whom he had chanced upon in a coffee shop at Winchmore Hill, London. Lorford told Mures that since January he had been lodging at Ridge Street, Watford, under the name of Harry Lee. He had been working at the Cocoa Factory, then at a printing works at Callowland, which was true. Not unnaturally, Mures enquired if he had heard about the Bricket Wood murder. 'Yes,' Lorford replied, 'I have been working near there and they don't seem to know who did it.' Later he told Mures, 'I could get ten years if I were to tell you a certain thing I have done.' 'What is that?' Mures asked. 'That is nothing to do with you,' said Lorford.

That June, Lorford was sentenced to 3 years' borstal training for an unconnected crime. On the 28th June he asked to see the Governor at Rochester Borstal 'to make a statement with reference to a crime I have committed'. In this statement, made voluntarily, he said:

'On December 26th I absconded from Redhill Farm School. I lived at Watford from January until May. I left Watford in the beginning of May and went to Brighton. I stole a revolver and 23 cartridges from the military rifle range in the Lower Esplanade. I walked back to Watford and on arrival I had no money or food. Next morning I was walking along the Watford–St Albans main road and saw Miss J. Oven coming along. I went up the Bricket Wood lane and when she came up I asked her for some money. I held the pistol up and she tried to snatch at it and the trigger went off. Two days after I returned the revolver and cartridges to the military rifle range, Brighton.'

His reference to 'Miss J. Oven' did not mean that he knew her identity at the time, but indicated that he did when he made the statement.

On 19th July, Lorford made another statement, this time to Superintendent Peck of St Albans police. In this one he gave an account of his lodging at Ridge Street, and admitted that he left suddenly after being discovered by his landlady in a bedroom where he shouldn't have been. Some articles went missing, as well as Lorford himself. In a third statement, he said, 'I can show you where I hid the black bag. I had a big black coat on at the time, and I left that in one place in the wood and the bag in another. I have taken everything out of the bag except seven pence in coppers.' In yet another statement, he said, 'She snatched at the revolver. I did not mean to shoot her. She fell to the ground and the second was in the neck. I dragged her into the ditch by her hands.' After that the police took Lorford to the woods where he indicated the spot where the coat was found and a bush where he said he had left the bag. The police had not found it, nor could they find it even when Lorford indicated the spot. But it was there, just as he said, hidden in the undergrowth.

Lorford's account of the burglary at what was in fact a shooting gallery at Brighton was corroborated by Annie Eva Stillwell, who worked there. She had gone to work on the morning in question to find that someone had entered by a window. A large cigarettes case had been broken into and the revolver and cartridges and some money had been stolen. Later, the stolen revolver and some ammunition had been unexpectedly returned by being slipped under the door. Lorford's account of everything: the burglary and theft of the gun and ammunition at Brighton, the killing of Janet Oven and subsequent disposal of clothing and property – only he could have known of the whereabouts of the handbag – was accurate. He was Janet's killer, but had he murdered her?

It was what Albert Lorford had to say, rather than what the prosecution could prove, that became material. Giving evidence, Lorford said that he slept in Cassiobury Park, Watford, on the night before he killed Janet. Next morning he walked along St Albans Road, carrying the revolver *with the hammer cocked*. How unusual, for someone to carry a gun with the hammer cocked; but that is what Lorford said, and who could say different? He admitted seeing Janet in Mount Pleasant Lane. 'Suddenly I thought I would stop her for some money,' he said. 'I waited until she was about three feet away, pulled the revolver out of my pocket and said, "Have you any money?" Almost before I had the words out of my mouth she snatched at the revolver and caught hold of it. She tried to pull it out of my hand. I tried to pull it back and the revolver fired as my finger caught on the trigger.' He still had to account for firing twice: 'She fell down flat on her face. I opened the revolver to take the empty cartridge out and as I opened it halfway I shut it and was holding it towards the ground when it went off...'

When asked about carrying a gun with the hammer cocked, Lorford could give no reason. Nor did he admit intending to hold anyone up that morning. He had merely asked Janet for money whilst pointing a cocked and loaded gun at her. His defence was that he had not intended to injure her.

So, the first shot was unintentional and occurred when Janet grabbed at the already-cocked revolver, and the second was an accident. He had never actually intended to injure his victim, he said. He was asking the jury to believe that having shot someone, he remained at the scene to take the empty cartridge out. But would a man remain at the scene of a crime to remove an empty cartridge from the gun with which he had shot his victim? Very doubtful, surely, and more likely it was that if the first shot was discharged unintentionally, or by Janet snatching at the gun as Lorford maintained, the second was premeditated, designed to finish her off, thus preventing her from ever identifying him as her attacker.

The second shot would thus be the one that killed her, fired at such close range that traces of gunpowder were deposited on her skin. If so, Albert Edward Lorford killed Janet Oven in cold blood. Yet the jury found him not guilty of murder, but guilty of manslaughter. Maybe they decided that a young man of sixteen in wartime England who was down on his luck, without means and maybe without family, who had voluntarily admitted his crime, deserved a break. Passing sentence, the Judge said, 'The jury have acquitted you of murder and found you guilty of the lesser offence of manslaughter. It is as near as murder as may be. You are not a lad of good character, but I take into consideration your youth. If you were a grown man I should give you at least double the sentence I am giving you. You must go to penal servitude for seven years.'

The Verdict

Was justice done in this case? Perhaps. After all, had Lorford not confessed, he would probably never have been caught. But had the letter of the law been observed? Hardly.

Albert Lorford had been seen hanging about over several mornings, and wasn't it the case that finally he got the nerve to rob Janet Oven on her way to work? Sleeping rough, as he was, he would have needed money. But did he shoot her deliberately? He said she 'snatched at the gun', which was cocked, ready to fire. Maybe she did, and if so who could blame her? One moment she was walking to work, reading her novel, the next there was someone pointing a gun at her head. She reacted as she did, without time to apply thought or reason. The responsibility for her death was his, nor hers. Janet Oven lies in the churchyard at All Saints Church, Leavesden, in an unmarked grave. A 'large crowd' attended the funeral of a young woman, murdered in her prime. Yes, murdered. Can there be any other verdict?

6

Redbourn 1921

"I didn't hardly know what I was doing"

Donald Litton – Child, Killer

It was just a routine visit. Jessie Freeman was calling on her mother, 71-year-old Sarah Seabrook, at her cottage at North Common, Redbourn. Jessie lived on the High Street, not far off, and her mother had suffered at least two seizures, since when she was having constant headaches and she was under the doctor. There was, too, the worrying problem of money going missing from the house. This was a mystery, and it had kept recurring, even when her mother locked herself in when Jessie left.

That morning, Thursday, 27th January, Jessie had called on her mother at 9.30. She was pleased to find her in better health than of late. Jessie cooked dinner, and as she was leaving to meet her husband in Harpenden she saw her two sisters arriving. They lived with their mother, but were out at work through the day. Mrs Seabrook saw Jessie to the gate and waved goodbye, Jessie no doubt reminding her to take her after-dinner nap as she always did – after locking herself in, of course.

At 3.30 that same afternoon Jessie returned. Her sisters would have gone back to work, so she was dutifully checking on her mother again. The front door was still locked, but she thought nothing amiss; her mother would be asleep upstairs on her bed. But when Jessie looked in the window and saw the room was filled with smoke, she became alarmed and returned to the front door which she managed to open. At once she saw that the smoke was coming from the kitchen, where she discovered a chair was on fire. Some clothes hanging on the back of the chair in front of the fire had caught alight and set fire to the chair. She threw the burning chair and clothing into the back garden and held the door open. One can imagine the scene as she stood by the open door and waited for the smoke to clear, thinking, perhaps, how fortunate it was that she had called when she did.

As she waited, Jessie heard a strange, gurgling sound. It seemed to come from somewhere between the doorpost and the sink. In the smoke she was unable to see anything, but bending down she found her mother lying on the floor with her back against the wall. Her face was covered in blood, her right arm was leaning on a pail of water and blood was flowing from her head, which rested against her arm, and was dripping into the water. Her mother murmured 'Jessie, Jessie,' and as she did 'thick bubbles of blood' came out of her mouth. Jessie noticed a poker lying on the floor in the middle of the room. It was bent double, although it had been perfectly straight when she had called at the house that morning.

Jessie went outside and called on a neighbour, Mrs Litton. Donald Litton, aged 13 years, who lived with his mother in the next cottage but one, came to the door and said his mother was not in. Jessie noticed that young Donald was wearing a day shirt but no trousers or coat. She then sought the help of another neighbour, Mrs Bradshaw, who helped her to take Mrs Seabrook out into the back garden, by which time other neighbours arrived at the house. It seems that Jessie thought her mother had suffered a seizure and the fire had been an accident.

Angela Moore, District Nurse, lived nearby, in Fish Street. She was sent for and arrived at Mrs Seabrook's cottage at 3.45. Her account, given at the inquest at West Herts Hospital, Hemel Hempstead, quickly dispelled any notion of illness or accident on the part of Mrs

Front View of the Cottage, with police on guard, together with dog (also inset) which was out at the time of the tragedy, but which is reported to have refused to leave the cottage since. [Illustrations by courtesy of "The

The scene of the crime

Illustrated Police News

Seabrook. As Nurse Moore passed through the kitchen she saw blood on the wall above the sink, and blood on and in two buckets nearby. There was blood on an enamel bowl, turned upside down in the sink, and on the window ledge. She saw that Mrs Seabrook had deep gashes on both temples and another in the middle of her forehead. She bound up these wounds. There was another injury to her left hand, near the thumb. Sitting on a chair, Mrs Seabrook kept repeating,

'Don't hurt me,' and 'Don't let him hurt me.'

Nurse Moore asked if she might see Mrs Seabrook's room. There she saw an impression on the bed, where Mrs Seabrook had been lying. There was an overturned table near the window, and the curtain was torn. There was blood on the floor beneath the window and a pool of blood beside the bed. There was more blood on the iron frame of the bed and on the sheet. There were bloody footprints on the landing, made by someone not wearing shoes. Nurse Moore was certain Mrs Seabrook had been attacked and seriously wounded, and estimated it had happened between half an hour and three-quarters of an hour before. A car was summonsed and Nurse Moore accompanied Mrs Seabrook to West Herts Hospital. On the journey Mrs Seabrook kept pushing an imaginary person away and kept repeating, 'Let me get up.'

Dr Georgina Davidson, House Surgeon, attended to Mrs Seabrook, who by now was unconscious. She discovered that she had five wounds to her forehead and at least eleven on top and to the sides of her head. There was a severe wound to her left ear. There were at least eight fractures to bones about Mrs Seabrook's person. Sarah Seabrook died in hospital of her injuries, not, as her daughter Jessie had suspected, of seizure or other illness, but as a result of being repeatedly struck with one or more heavy objects. She had been brutally murdered in her home. But by whom? And why? No-one knew, and the inquest into Mrs Seabrook's tragic death was adjourned until 11th February.

It was Dr Davidson who called the police, but before they arrived well meaning neighbours cleaned up the blood and tidied up the house. It may be that the police did not have the means to attend quickly then, for today a crime scene is sealed for careful forensic examination. Any clues were thus destroyed or lost, save for the bent

RIGHT **"Found with terrible head injuries"**
How Sarah Seabrook was found in her cottage at Redbourn, 1921
Illustrated Police News

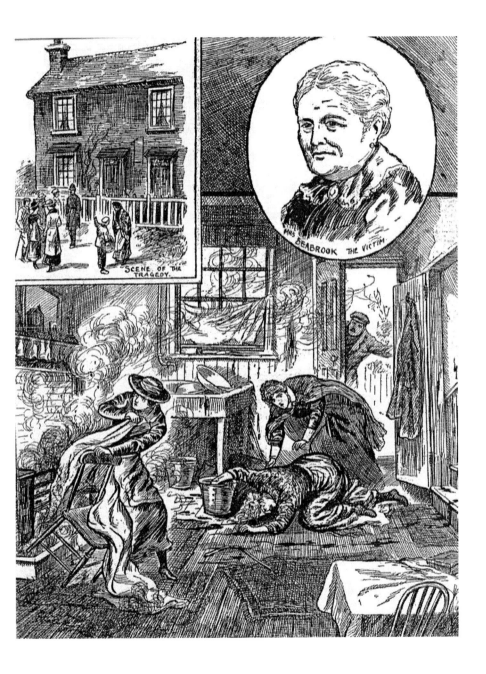

SCENE OF THE TRAGEDY.

MRS SEABROOK THE VICTIM.

poker, found on the kitchen floor, which Jessie Freeman and her sisters were adamant had not been bent that morning. There appeared to be no obvious motive. No money was apparently missing, and none of Mrs Seabrook's family could think of any enemies their mother could possibly have had.

As well as Hertfordshire detectives being assigned to the case, Scotland Yard was called in. Today, one might wonder why this was so, why someone with no knowledge of the area and who was unknown to police personnel there should be introduced to the enquiry. The Yard, apparently, had the expertise. The Yard's man was Detective Inspector Crutchet. Another was Sergeant William McBride, who took photographs of the cottage and of Mrs Seabrook, showing her injuries. They hadn't far to look for the killer. A week later the *Hertfordshire Advertiser* reported that, 'Late on Wednesday evening, in the darkness, a motor car pulled up at the door of the police station in Victoria Street, St Albans. The figures who emerged were not recognisable, but it was clear one of them was a lad, a mere stripling who was lodged in the police station for the night'. So it was. He was Donald Litton, the 13-year-old boy from just two doors away.

Master Litton appeared before a specially convened Children's Court at St Albans the following morning. He was described as, 'a mere schoolboy in knickerbocker suit and Eton collar, with his right knee bandaged, wearing an overcoat and carrying his cap in his hand. He seemed remarkably self-possessed for a boy of his years, somewhat over average height and his round, pallid face bears the unmistakable stamp of intelligence'. After being formally charged with murder the court was told that Litton had made a voluntary statement of admission and he was remanded in custody until Saturday. Litton avoided eye contact with the magistrates, staring throughout at the chandelier on the ceiling.

When Donald Litton next appeared on remand, the court's first concern was whether or not he could be tried for the crime at all. He was a boy of thirteen, so could he be sent for trial? The law was clear: a child under the age of seven years could not be convicted of any crime; over seven and under fourteen he was 'presumed to be incapable of committing crime, unless there was evidence that he had understanding and discretion in the ordinary circumstances of life which would indicate intelligence beyond his years'. In short, it was for the prosecution to prove he was intelligent enough to know the consequences of his actions.

Testifying, Det Insp Crutchet said that the police investigation had involved interviewing local people. Donald Litton was one of these, and in an initial statement he made to the police, two days after the murder, he stated that he lived with his widowed mother, Lizzie Alice Litton, at North Common, Redbourn. On Wednesday 26th January (the day before the murder) he was playing with another boy when he fell and cut his knee. It was attended to by school staff, and later the same day by his mother, who re-bandaged it. Consequently he was off school on the Thursday. On that day he said he played in the back garden during the morning, and after two o'clock his mother went out. He said that at about 2.15 he went to the well (situated in the garden) to draw water. Forgetting his knee was stiff, and on the slippery woodwork, he slipped into the well. He managed to keep his head above the water, and was able to climb out by pressing his feet and back against the sides and by pressing his hands on the bricks underneath him. He went indoors, took his clothes off and put them into the bath with his boots. Then he sat in front of the fire wearing only his shirt. Said the prosecution of this statement, 'It might have been a fairy tale.'

Mrs Litton said when she got home she found Donald sitting in the front room. Asked what he was wearing, she replied, 'He had got knickers and a nightshirt on.' He was sitting in front of the fire. When she asked him why he was so dressed, he said he had fallen down the well. The well served three cottages and there was only a lid on the top. She saw that his clothing, including his boots, were in the bath. There was no water in the bath at that time but the clothes and boots were wet. She had since washed his clothing. She added that the teachers at school were going to take some boys to the zoo, provided they could pay seven shillings. She agreed her son was a 'sharp boy'.

Donald Litton's first statement was one of many made by local residents to the police, not one of someone who was under suspicion. It concerned his account of hurting his knee and falling down the well. But the police were suspicious, and four days later they asked him to go to Redbourn police station to make another statement, 'as there were certain facts to clear up'. There certainly were. Detective Sergeant Askew of Scotland Yard said that on the way to the police station, Litton said, 'If I told the truth, will I get a summons?' The policeman said, 'We can make no promises to you.' (How many times do investigating detectives utter those words in their career?). Litton: 'My only worry is if my mother gets to know. I killed Mrs Seabrook.' He admitted hitting her first with a hammer, which he had buried in the garden, then the poker. The hammer, which police recovered, was identified by Mrs Litton's lodger, Charles Ford, who said it was usually kept in their barn.

On 2nd February, Litton made a second statement, which he wrote down himself. Two policemen 'stood nearby' as he did so. 'Nothing was said to the prisoner during the time he was writing this statement,' said Det Insp Crutchet. Donald Litton was unaccompanied by an adult and had no legal representation, so today any such statement would be inadmissible. As to the police 'saying nothing' when it was written, the jury would have to take their word for it.

A resume of Donald Litton's second statement reads as follows:

'On 27th January I went up the garden and came back just after 2 o'clock. My mother had just gone out. I wanted some money to go to the zoo at Easter. I went to the barn and got a hammer. I went to Mrs Seabrook's back door and tried it. It was bolted. I pulled the window down and opened the door. I looked in the kitchen and front room but I couldn't find any money. I went upstairs into the back room. There was no-one there. I opened the other door slowly and looked in. Mrs Seabrook woke up and saw the door open. She got out of bed and came to the door. I was frightened and I struck her on the head with the hammer. This was in the front room, in the doorway. She ran to the window and tried to open it. I caught her wrist and pulled her back on the floor. She knocked over the small table. I hit her with the hammer. Then I ran downstairs and up the garden and buried the hammer in Miss Weston's garden. I went to her house again. She was coming downstairs. I pushed her over and she tried to get up again. I picked up the poker and struck her with it. She kept trying to get up and I struck her with the poker. The chair fell on the fire. I ran out and got down the well. I didn't hardly know what I was doing. I thought I would drown myself.'

Litton went on to again give account of how he got into and climbed out of the well, then going home and taking his clothes off and putting them into a pail. 'At 3.30 Mrs Freeman knocked on our front window. She called out, "Mrs Litton." I said "Mother isn't in." She went to the wall and called, "Police!" '. Then he saw Mr and Mrs Bradshaw and other neighbours, and watched the car take Mrs Seabrook away. Comment was then made that Donald Litton was undefended in court. Nonetheless, he was remanded in custody to face trial. No mention was made, then or later, of the mystery of the missing money at Mrs Seabrook's cottage. In all probability this was Litton, too, but pilfering took a back seat against a charge of murder.

The second inquest was held at the Town Hall, in what is now Hemel Hempstead Old Town. Litton was brought from Boxmoor railway station by 'public motor bus' (having been in Brixton prison). Much of the same evidence of the first inquest was heard, except having had a post mortem the jury was told of the specific and gruesome injuries to Mrs Seabrook.

Old Town Hall, Hemel Hempstead
Scene of the resumed inquest into the murder of Mrs Sarah Seabrook

Dr Gilroy carried out the post mortem examination. The injury list was long and harrowing. To summarise: there were 28 wounds to her scalp of varying degrees of severity, many of them fracturing the skull. Her left forearm and hand were also fractured, as well as other injuries consistent with a savage, sustained attack. The cause of death was 'shock from loss of blood consequent upon the injuries to the head'. The injuries had been caused by another person and could not have been self-inflicted. The poker could have caused most, but not all of these injuries. There were others that had been caused by a broad shaped object, such as the head of a hammer. Many of the wounds had been inflicted upon Mrs Seabrook when she was unconscious. Her arm and hand were probably injured as she tried to defend herself. On that quiet afternoon in sleepy Redbourn, Donald Litton had entered

SATURDAY, FEBRUARY 19, 1921.

REDBOURN MURDER CHARGE.

ADJOURNED POLICE COURT PROCEEDINGS.

FURTHER EVIDENCE OF COTTAGE CRIME.

BENT POKER PRODUCED IN COURT.

DONALD LITTON'S FIRST STATEMENT.

HIS MOTHER IN WITNESS BOX.

The remand hearing of the case in which the boy Donald Litton, aged thirteen, of Redbourn, is accused of the wilful murder of Mrs. Sarah Seabrook, a widow, aged 71, at her cottage at [...] on [...] January 27th [...]

opinion, it was sufficient evidence to rebut the presumption to which he had referred—that the boy was incapable of committing such a crime. There were other facts in the case, one of them being that the boy washed his clothes immediately after the occurrence, and that fact was im- [...]

an old lady's house and meted out the most cruel and merciless attack upon her person. It was, by any measure, a murder most foul.

Det Insp Crutchet said that Litton's written confession had been written without any suggestion of composition, punctuation or spelling from him. This was an important point, considering Litton's 'tender years'. When asked whether he thought it would be possible for Litton to get out of the well, the officer said, 'I should doubt it.' The well was 27 feet deep, which included ten feet of water, and was very narrow. Maybe the police considered the account of the well to be false, that in truth Litton had simply washed his clothes in the bath. But Mrs Litton said there was grit and brick dust on his clothing, and his boots were 'red with brick dust'. In any event the verdict of the jury was that Sarah Seabrook had been murdered by Donald Litton.

Redbourn today

The trial of Donald Litton took place at the Hertfordshire Assizes that June. Master Litton wore a smart suit and was described as 'looking well though a little pale, and perfectly collected in his demeanour'. He pleaded Not Guilty to the murder of Sarah Seabrook. This was not a denial that he had killed her, but an attempt by his defence to have the case dismissed on account of his age. The judge was Justice Sydney Rowlatt.

Mr Cecil Whiteley, for the prosecution, pointed out that Donald Litton was now fourteen years of age, but was 13½ when he killed Mrs Seabrook. He said that if the person charged was between 7 and 14 at the time of the crime, as Litton was, the law presumed him incapable of criminal intent; so to convict him the prosecution would seek to satisfy the jury he was capable of 'criminal intention'.

Mr A. Leighton appeared for Litton. He agreed Litton had killed Mrs Seabrook, but the jury would have to consider whether he had 'guilty knowledge'. 'The question is whether the defendant actually set out to commit this deed,' he said. 'He went to the house knowing he had no business there and became frightened when Mrs Seabrook came towards him, and struck her with the hammer. After leaving the house he returned and seeing Mrs Seabrook coming down the stairs he became temporality bereft of his thoughts. The boy did not realise what he was doing. He could not have been capable of committing the crime having regard to his age, and there was nothing to prove he had anything but ordinary intelligence of a boy of that age, and nothing in his character to lead one to suppose that he was naturally of criminal instinct or intention.'

Summing up, the Judge referred to Litton's age, and the question of 'guilty knowledge', the only part of the case that was relevant in deciding guilt or otherwise. He then reviewed the evidence and informed the jury they had to consider whether Donald Litton had the understanding to make him guilty. After deliberating for three minutes the jury returned a guilty verdict. Being under 16 years of age he could not be sentenced to death. Instead, he was sentenced to be detained 'during His Majesty's Pleasure'. Proceedings ended on a bizarre note when the Judge, referring to a letter he had received from a 'certain person', said he did not have the power to allow Donald Litton to be adopted. Did he believe that if he had the power to do this, and had done so, that the public would have been adequately protected?

"A judge knows nothing unless it has been explained to him three times"

(English proverb)

What are the qualities a judge needs to sit in judgement? Whatever they are, is it right that one person alone, however learned, should judge another who is charged with a criminal offence? Whatever their eminence, judges are human beings with human traits. Like anyone else they have moods, good and bad; they have problems,

---

The Verdict

'The boy became frightened when Mrs Seabrook came towards him, and struck her with the hammer. After leaving the house he returned and seeing Mrs Seabrook coming down the stairs he became temporarily bereft of his thoughts. The boy did not realise what he was doing...'

These were the words of defence counsel, in his endeavour to make the case that Donald Litton was Not Guilty of murdering Sarah Seabrook. Yet Donald Litton went to the house of someone he knew was old and frail, taking with him a hammer which he used when Mrs Seabrook saw him at her bedroom door. He hit her on the head with it, at least twice, and returned to beat her mercilessly with a poker, so severely it was bent double. Didn't realise what he was doing? The only surprise in this case was that the jury took all of three minutes to find him guilty. He was detained during His Majesty's Pleasure. Alas, there is no record of how long this actually was. Wouldn't it be nice to know?

---

anything from sciatica to fractious relations with the in-laws. Justice Rowlatt certainly seemed to get out of bed on the wrong side on the day Donald Litton stood in the dock. This was a tragic case, a 13-year-old boy robbing and murdering a 71-year-old woman. How did the eminent Judge conduct himself at the Assizes that day? Not very commendably. Here is an extract, verbatim, from what he had to say when the prosecution introduced evidence of the photographs, taken by police, of Mrs Seabrook's cottage:

'What is this? Just an ordinary home, a common cottage. I think it is a waste of public money. Fancy having these elaborate photographs just to lock up a naughty boy. It has nothing to do with the case.' One wonders what Mrs Seabrook's bereaved family thought of those words.

Again, when the prosecution said they would call George Freeman to prove identification of his mother-in-law's body: 'Is there any doubt as to her identity?' and on being told there was not: 'Go away, Freeman. It is a perfect waste and it is unnecessary. I have tried hundreds of murder cases and it is only in this part of the country that this kind of thing is happening.' He wasn't finished. When the bent poker was handed to May Seabrook: 'That thing was photographed too. There it is, gentlemen. You have seen a photograph of a poker and now you see the poker as well.'

Is it possible for judgement to be impaired when someone is so insensitive? If so, maybe a panel of three should sit in judgement. Then, hopefully, with personal prejudices omitted, a more rational approach may be made when deciding what is and is not relevant to the case, and what is and is not fair.

Hertfordshire Hemel Hempstead Gazette
& WEST HERTS ADVERTISER

No. 4704   ESTABLISHED 1856   FRIDAY, SEPTEMBER 21, 1956.   TELEPHONE: BOXMOOR 1472/74   Registered as a Newspaper for transmission in the United Kingdom and Abroad.   3d.

HUNT FOR MURDERER INTENSIFIED

Kings Langley Man Burned

Car Identification Parade Makes History

7

The 'Kid Gloves' Murder

Near Leverstock Green 1956

Two Murder Hunt 'Firsts'

The quiet, narrow lanes to the east of Hemel Hempstead are largely unchanged over the years, save for the MI motorway which was driven through their midst over forty years ago, and the widening of Green Lane off Breakespear Way, which serviced the Buncefield oil terminal. Today, Hogg End Lane is much the same as it ever was, a quiet link between Green Lane and the A5183, the former A5. On these quiet byways, on a quiet September afternoon in 1956, murder was committed. Murderer and victim were seen by several witnesses, both before and possibly during the deed, and immediately after it, yet despite the best efforts of police no-one was ever apprehended. The investigation would include two 'firsts': a 'portrait' of the suspect, fashioned from the description given by a witness, and an identification parade, not of suspects but of motor cars.

It was about 2.50 p.m. on a Friday when three schoolboy cyclists from Adeyfield noticed a car parked in Green Lane. They were Alan Glaister, aged 13, Nicholas Heaslewood, 14, and Allen Clarke, also 14, who lived at Wealdstone but was staying at his grandmother's. There could be no obvious reason why anyone should stop in such a place, and so intrigued were they that they hid their bicycles in the hedge, and kept watch from a distance. They saw the driver walking away from the car. He was carrying something which he dumped into the bracken, three feet high, at the roadside. It might have been rubbish, but when the man drove off one of the boys said he thought it might have been 'a body', which made them all laugh. Then they poked the bundle with a stick and thought they saw a leg, after which they cycled away as fast as they could and perchance they saw a policeman.

When the policeman looked closely at the bundle he told the boys to cycle to a telephone box and call the police station. A police car arrived, and the boys were taken to the police station to make statements. When they arrived home late for their tea their parents threatened to stop their pocket money. But events took on a more serious tone when they were told that the boys had discovered the partly-clothed body of a woman, who minutes before had been strangled and dumped in the bracken by the driver of the car.

She was identified as Diana Winifred Suttey, aged 36, a married woman from Harrow. She had been strangled with a pink and white scarf, and there were teeth marks on her body. Although married, she did not live with her husband, Charles Suttey, 28, who lived in London. It was he who identified her body, and police were satisfied he had not seen her for a fortnight. Mrs Suttey was also known by her previous married name, Ledger, and her maiden name, Morgan. That her body had been found immediately was most fortuitous, for without the observations of the three passing schoolboys she may have laid undetected for weeks or months, longer even.

The boys had most assiduously noted the description of the man who dumped the body, describing him as about 50 years of age, 5 feet 8 inches tall with dark hair, greying at the sides, and of medium height, wearing a navy blue pin-striped suit, horn-rimmed glasses with thick lenses and brown or yellow kid gloves. They also took note of the description of the car, which they thought to be a light grey or pastel Standard 8 or 10, registered number possibly SUU 138. It was fortunate that the man did not notice that he was being watched, or if he did he was in such a panic that he sought only to get away. He may have reacted violently to anyone he believed able to identify him, given that he had just committed murder, a capital crime then.

The officer sent to head the investigation was Detective Superintendent Albert Griffin of Scotland Yard, who had earlier worked on the infamous Christie case. He, together with Hertfordshire detectives, commenced enquiries. First, there was the examination of the place where Mrs Suttey's body had been dumped, which included the attendance at the scene of the eminent Home Office pathologist, Dr Keith Simpson. The media were quick to report the incident, including the London *Evening Standard*, which reported dramatically that 'Detectives from the Yard had visited mist-shrouded Green Lane…'.

Police established that Mrs Suttey was known to frequent transport cafes in the Markyate area, where she was known to lorry drivers and other men of the road. As early as the night of the murder they were focusing their enquiries in Watling Street, the former A5, where a lorry driver told them he had seen Mrs Suttey, whom he knew, accept a lift from a man driving a two-tone grey Rover car, about 2.30 p.m., near the Crow's Nest café, between Markyate and Redbourn. It seems the police were satisfied this was not the same vehicle seen shortly

afterwards in Green Lane, but they sought the driver nonetheless. The next morning, they searched the scene, looking for Mrs Suttey's handbag, which may have contained documents giving clues to her killer's identity, and one of her brown shoes, which was missing. They cut away the long undergrowth with billhooks, but found neither item nor anything else. Plaster cast impressions were taken of tyre marks on the grass verges. Further impressions were taken of teeth marks found on Mrs Suttey's body. A reconstruction of teeth was later published in the British Dental Journal in an attempt to find a match to identify the killer. Teeth marks are as identifiable as fingerprints, each being unique to one person.

A Central Murder Office was set up at Hemel Hempstead police station, a sort of forerunner to today's incident room system. The police had acted quickly and were doing all the right things. One of these was to check out the registered number of the car. It turned out to be either false or mistakenly taken, as it came down to a three-wheeler. This was a bitter blow. They would have considered a similar registered number, but unlike today, where a computer check quickly identifies the owner of a motor vehicle, searches then had to be done painstakingly, a slow, methodical process involving checking card indices at county halls and town halls where details were kept. Some 107,000 numbers were reportedly checked, which failed to provide the sought-after result.

The police appealed for witnesses to come forward, and there were plenty who did, a quite astonishing fact considering the remote location where events took place. The three schoolboys who saw the man dump Mrs Suttey's body were not alone in witnessing events that afternoon. Two other 14-year-old boys, who were on a cycling trip from Harrow, came forward. They reported that about ten minutes earlier they had seen a smartly dressed man and a woman in the back seat of a car parked in Hogg End Lane, about a mile away from where the body was dumped. The man was bending over the woman, they said.

Thomas Owen, a farmer, of Kettlewell's Farm, said he saw a man and a woman in a grey car being driven along Hogg End Lane towards Green Lane. Mrs Freda Fitzjohn, wife of the head cowman at Kettlewell's Farm, not only saw a car, but spoke to the occupants. She was taking her two children, aged 3 years and fifteen months, for a walk along Hogg End Lane shortly before 3 o'clock. The children were in a pram. The Fitzjohns' black Labrador ran into the front of the car, which had to slow down or stop. Mrs Fitzjohn spoke to the driver, intending to apologise, and saw that there was also a woman in the car. She said the driver 'stared vacantly' at her, and that neither occupant spoke to her at all. She did not take much notice of the woman.

William Steer, 23, a van driver from Pimilico, near Leverstock Green, approached a car travelling in the opposite direction along Hogg End Lane and had to reverse his van to allow the car to pass. The driver called out, 'I'm all right.' It would be shortly after this that the car was seen in Green lane, and 15-year-old Barbara Seeby, from Leverstock Green and her friend, Barry Hughes, said they saw a bluey-green car in Green Lane just after 3 o'clock. It was unoccupied at that time. The schoolboys who were keeping observations shouted at them, but they took no notice. They must have happened along as the murderer was dumping Mrs Suttey's body in the bracken.

Detectives considered Mrs Fitzjohn's close encounter with the man and woman in a car in Hogg End Lane to be vital in their effort to identify the man, almost certainly the murderer. She was taken to a police artist's studio in Chelsea, her account of which appeared in the *Hemel Hempstead Gazette*:

'I was shown a large number of photographs which had been cut into small pieces. These were fitted together like a jig-saw puzzle, and from the result the artist made charcoal drawings. These were also cut into small pieces and another jig-saw portrait was made. I then gave advice from which another, completed portrait, was drawn.' It is believed that this was the first time in the annals of British crime detection such a portrait had been prepared. The 'portrait' was published in *Police Gazette*, and circulated to all forces.

The police were satisfied that the unknown driver of the Rover car had given Mrs Suttey a genuine lift along Watling Street, but continued to appeal for him to come forward. Genuine or not, he never did, and they never traced him. Meanwhile, they continued their search to identify the car so many had seen in the vicinity. To identify the car was almost certain to identify the murderer. Its make was uncertain, the registered number was incorrect, but to identify it was vital. To do so, they formed an 'identification parade' of cars.

It took place in Gadebridge Road, Hemel Hempstead. A line-up of some 40–60 cars, kindly provided by local dealers and residents, stretched for 200 yards along the road, and one by one the witnesses, each accompanied by a detective, walked the line. The objective was to establish the make and colour of the suspect's car. The cars were of various shades of grey and green and fawn, and included some American models and Volkswagens, which were rare in those days. The parade was confined to police and witnesses, and the press. It lasted over an hour after which the Chief Constable, Lieut. Colonel Wilcox, thanked all those who had taken part. After the parade, the police were able to say that the suspect car was probably a Standard 8 or 10, or maybe a Morris, possibly of medium blue-green or blue-grey and not of lighter colour as at first thought. The search field had 'decreased' to some 250,000 cars. It would take time to check out the owners. They failed, but one cannot fault the enterprise of Superintendent Griffin and his team. It is believed that the motor car 'identification parade' was the first to be held in the country.

There were other lines of enquiries, during the course of which the police sought a man who had stayed at an hotel in Hemel Hempstead and who left on the date of the murder, earlier than expected. They did not trace him. They visited at least two car factories in the Midlands. As well as 'thousands' of motorists, suspects interviewed included two gypsies from Saffron Walden who were in the area at the time of the

Scene of crime
Hogg End Lane is little changed

murder, a number of schoolteachers, a large number of commercial travellers and three clergymen. All were alibied. Other enquiries were made as far afield as Oxford and Newcastle upon Tyne, all to no avail. Of Mrs Suttey herself, it was established that she had previously been engaged in domestic employment, and efforts were made to trace former employers in the Stanmore and Elstree areas. Whatever success the police had in this regard, it did not provide any positive lead. Nor did their check of dental records. 'All the latest scientific knowledge was used' to trace the murderer or his car. As the *Gazette* reported: 'Enquiries are being conducted in the way that a master chess player solves a difficult problem on the board'. Alas, it ended in stalemate. Despite the number of people who saw both murderer and

The Verdict

There can be no verdict in a case where there was no trial. Which is not to say that conclusions cannot be drawn.

Diana Suttey was estranged from her husband and, for reasons known to herself, seemed to be 'a woman of the road'. She was known in transport cafés, at least along the A5, and regularly accepted lifts from lorry drivers and strange men in strange cars. What was she about, then? Practising the oldest profession? Or simply occupying her time, seeking whatever company she could? Whatever her lifestyle, she ended up strangled in the country lanes near Hemel Hempstead, the victim of a sexual attack, her body thrown into the bracken by her killer.

One feels that this was a woman living a wretched life, not perhaps directly through choice but rather as a victim of circumstance. A waif, a stray, a leaf in the breeze. There are many who might say she had it coming: what could she expect, carrying on like that? In fact, she had every right not to expect 'she had it coming'. The worst that can be said of her is that she was foolish; the best that she did not deserve her fate. No-one 'deserves' to be murdered. As for the police, they did everything possible to track down the man who took her life. They exhausted all possible lines of enquiries. That's all society can expect.

Potters Bar 1955

Murder on the Golf Course

Mrs Elizabeth Currell, aged 46, lived at Cranborne Road, Potters Bar. About eight o'clock on the evening of Friday, 29th April, 1955, she left her house to take the family dog for a walk. As she walked on the nearby golf course, she encountered someone who struck her on the head with a tee-iron, a short, heavy metal post with a rectangular metal plate attached. It was a vicious and sustained attack, during which Mrs Currell was stripped of her clothing, and one or more attempts were made to strangle her before she was beaten to death. Her bloodstained assailant fled, leaving her battered body to be discovered the next day.

Police immediately put the fear of God into the population by declaring, albeit truthfully, that they thought the killer was probably a local man. It was no surprise to find women ensuring they never ventured anywhere alone, and who could blame them? One woman declared, 'I am carrying a strip of iron in my handbag and a pot of pepper in my pocket when I go out.' The golf course, normally frequented by dog walkers and courting couples, especially during the evening, was deserted at sunset.

Police had an early breakthrough: a palm print was found on the murder weapon, the tee-iron. The identity of the person to whom it belonged was not known, and to find out police would visit over 7,000 houses and take the finger and palm prints of 7,531 men. As well as appealing locally for information, police turned to Interpol for help. The reply to Scotland Yard was that the murderer could be one and the same as 'The Beast of the Autobahn', who was believed to have murdered twenty women in Germany. There were similarities between these crimes and the murder of Mrs Currell: in all cases the victim had been unclothed, battered and possibly strangled. Whilst appreciating the information provided by their German counterparts, it would be doubtful if the Yard really believed the German 'Beast' had committed murder in Hertfordshire.

On 26th August the police identified their killer. He was an 18-year-old man, who was 17 at the time of the murder. He lived in Potters Bar, and worked in the Treasurer's department at the council. Det Supt Crawford, giving evidence at the hearing at Barnet Magistrates' Court, said that when he was arrested, the man said, 'I found her. She was dead.' When asked why he had not told the police, he replied, 'You would not believe me.' Then, after a pause, he added, 'I hit her then I tried to strangle her.'

If there was any doubt that he was Mrs Currell's killer, it was dispelled when he elected to make his own, written statement. In it, he detailed a dreadful catalogue of violence. He wrote, 'I saw her walking towards me with her dog. I waited until she was out of sight behind the trees. I ran up behind her and tried to knock her out. She struggled. I hit her on the jaw. Then I tried to strangle her. I thought she was dead and dragged her over to the hedge where I tried to interfere with her. She was still alive and I had to hit her with the tee-iron to kill her. I hit her until we were both covered in blood. Then I ran across the railway line and home through the wood. I remember while we were struggling she screamed and talked to her dog, which ran away. She said, "You silly boy. You will only get into trouble." I put my hands round her throat and tried to strangle her. Then I dragged her over to the hedge where I undressed her. I ripped off most of her underclothes.

'I pulled off one of her stockings and tied it round her neck. It broke and I hit her with a piece of wood. The wood broke as well so I hit her with the tee-iron. I hit her until I was sure she was dead. I wiped most of the blood on my clothes in the stream at the bottom of Bridgefoot Lane. I told my mother a few days later that I found Mrs Currell and picked her up to see if she was still alive, to explain the blood on my clothes.' The account is abridged and not quite chronological.

The statement was born out by the evidence: bloodstained pieces of wood, the clothing, the deceased's body and, not least, his palm print, or part of it, on the tee-iron. Giving evidence, his mother said that when she had taken a cup of tea to her son, in bed, the following morning, she saw his bloodstained clothes. Like any mother she was concerned. He said, 'Mum, don't fuss.' He then went to work. She must have known, or at least suspected, that her son was a killer, once the details of the murder became known. She did not go to the police. Can a mother's protective instincts be justified in such circumstances?

That October, he stood trial at the Old Bailey. That very morning, Mrs Currell's husband, Alfred, received a letter, delivered to his home. It was written by the man charged with his wife's murder, saying he would be pleading guilty to save Mr Currell the ordeal of going into the witness box. He did indeed plead 'guilty' to murder. His mother was called to 'prove' his date of birth, 5th July, 1937, a very relevant part of the proceedings.

Why did this young man commit this dreadful crime? It is true to say he had an unfortunate accident when he was thirteen when he lost an eye through being struck by a pellet from an air rifle. His injured eyeball was removed and replaced by a glass eye. That aside, it seems he was a normal lad, with an interest in motor cycles and walking. He was described as 'intelligent' and was one for 'shunning' girls, hardly surprising, perhaps. Maybe it was sexual frustration that drove him to attack a lone woman; he admitted 'interfering' with her, 1950's jargon for sexual assault. Frustration, rage, panic: who knows what caused him to murder? As for 'proving' his date of birth, this established that he was under eighteen years of age when he killed Mrs Currell. He missed being hanged by 66 days, and was detained 'during the Queen's pleasure'.

Miss Anne Noblett

8

Marshalls Heath 1957

The Murder of Anne Noblett

She was seventeen and shy, and had spent the afternoon at Lourdes Hall, Harpenden, learning to rock and roll. And afterwards, when she took the bus to Marshalls Heath, she would have just a 15-minute walk home, up the quiet lane where she lived with her parents. But Anne Noblett never arrived, and as time wore on her panic-stricken father telephoned friends and finally the police to report a missing person.

It was Monday, 30th December, 1957, and it was not like Anne to stay out without telling her parents. That she had been to the dance was not in doubt; she had been met by a friend, Annette Solway, and a girl called Isabel. Annette and Anne had danced together, then left with two other girls at 5.30 p.m. They walked along Southdown Road to Station Road, where they saw Anne's bus, the 391, pulling away. Anne said she would catch another bus at Church Field, and left her friends, saying she would see them on Friday.

Precisely which bus Anne caught is uncertain, but shortly after six o'clock it seems she got off a bus at Cherry Tree Corner on the Luton Road at Marshalls Heath, from where she would walk up Marshalls Heath Lane to her home. In the darkness of that late December evening she was seen by Shirley Edwards, who worked on a nearby poultry farm. Miss Edwards had left work at 6 p.m. and had driven down Marshalls Heath Lane on her scooter. She saw Anne walking slowly along the main road, as though to turn up the lane. She also noticed a bus pulling away. She and Anne had called out 'hello' to each another. A positive identification, then. It was the last time Anne was seen alive, except, that is, by her killer, or killers.

Mr Thomas Noblett, Anne's father, described his daughter as 'a quiet, home loving girl'. She was a domestic science student at Watford Technical College, and she had intended to become a children's nurse. She had no known 'male associates' and never stayed out late without telling her parents. Not that she had been out late on the night in question, but by 9 p.m., when she had not returned home, Mr Noblett picked up the telephone. Tragically, Anne's parents' fears would be realised, that something terrible had happened to their daughter; and what would make things worse would be the fact that they would never know what exactly, for the circumstances of Anne's murder, and what happened during the month thereafter before her body was discovered, has remained a mystery.

The next day, New Year's Eve, sixty police officers were searching for Anne. They combed the fields and woodlands, some using tracker dogs, and they dragged the River Lea, but there was no sign of her. They extended their search to cess-pits and wells, without success. By the Sunday after her disappearance the search team comprised 80 uniformed police officers who were joined by officers and men of Territorial Army units and cadet troops, as well as civilians who also provided transport. Areas already searched were searched again, then the searching was extended to include Blackmore End and Gustard Wood, Blackbridge refuse dump, Nomansland and Harpenden Commons, Rothamstead Park and Kinsbourne Green and Luton Hoo, which was searched by Bedfordshire Police. They checked unoccupied houses and other buildings, and garden sheds. They scoured the quiet lanes and lonely farms of the Hertfordshire countryside. They looked everywhere, but there was no sign of Anne.

The assistance given by the public was acknowledged by the Chief Constable, Mr A.F. Wilcox, who wrote to the *Hertfordshire Advertiser* to offer his thanks: 'It is impossible to speak too highly of the voluntary

The Herts Advertiser & St Albans Times

spirit of service shown by the large number of people who turned out individually and in organised bodies to take part in the search, especially when conditions were very bad.' The latter point was a reminder that this was the depths of winter, albeit a mild one.

Detective Superintendent Elwell was in charge. As well as co-ordinating the search and conducting other enquiries, he visited police in Essex, where a Dutch girl, Marie Kriek, had disappeared when in the vicinity of a bus stop. Miss Kriek had been found dead, but no link with Anne Noblett's disappearance was established.

The police desperately sought more witnesses, anyone who might have seen something: Anne walking up the lane, perhaps; or a stranger, or a strange car. They found one, a man who got off a Luton-bound bus near the Cherry Tree public house, just two or three minutes after Anne apparently got off hers. He had alighted with another man, and after talking to him briefly he walked up Marshalls Heath Lane for short distance, before turning along a footpath leading to the rear of the Lea Valley estate.

He told police that as he walked along the footpath he looked up the lane and saw two red lights. They were a few hundred yards away, and he was unable to tell if they were the rear lights of a car, or perhaps a motorcycle combination or even two bicycles. Nor could he tell whether or not they were moving. There was no sound, he said. Well, it was something. Perhaps it indicated a car was in the lane. If so, and it was connected, Anne could have been abducted, in which case she could be anywhere, miles away from the search scene perhaps. Which, as it turned out, she was, at least when she was found. But only just.

Anne's body was found in Young's Wood, Rose Grove Lane, about a mile and a half from Whitwell and about six miles from her home, on Friday, 31st January, 1958. The chance discovery was made by two brothers. They were a leading aircraftman in the R.A.F., aged 21, and his 14-year-old brother. Their dog had gone after a rabbit and the brothers went after it. In a clearing in the woods, about 300 yards from a muddy cart track running alongside the wood, they saw Anne. She was lying face upwards, fully clothed, wearing the same clothing she had worn when she had gone to the dance at Harpenden a month before. She was still wearing her spectacles and wrist watch.

There had been no attempt to conceal Anne's body. Her purse, containing about thirty shillings (£1.50) was found next to her. She had been asphyxiated, probably by strangulation, certainly by a violent act and not a self inflicted one, probably on the night of her disappearance. The evidence for this was the contents of her stomach, undigested food she had eaten shortly before her death. Crucially, although Anne was found fully clothed and wearing her overcoat, she had been stripped and re-dressed. This was proved by buttons on her underclothes being wrongly done up, a mistake she would not have made. There had been 'sexual interference', although exactly what was never disclosed. This was a crime scene. But was it a murder scene? Had Anne been murdered elsewhere and brought here afterwards?

Home Office pathologist, Dr Francis Camps, said that in his opinion Anne had been murdered soon after she disappeared. Her body had been in a frozen state for some time, even though the weather had been mild. The conclusion police drew from this was that after her murder Anne's body had been kept in deep-freeze conditions. Then, sometime before she was found, she had been taken to the woods and left on the ground, perhaps in the hope that everyone would believe she had died there. But the cause of death, asphyxiation, meant the truth was otherwise. It may be significant that her purse and money were found next to her, for these were the days shortly after a change in the law; where once you would hang for murder, now, under the provisions of the Homicide Act, 1957, you could hang for murder only in certain circumstances, one of which was murder in the furtherance of theft. Perhaps by ensuring her money was found, the killer – or killers – were ensuring they would not hang if apprehended.

The police investigation changed from a missing person enquiry to a murder enquiry, which meant, in those days, that the case would be taken over by a senior detective from Scotland Yard. Superintendent R. Lewis was on the case. 'Little pieces of the jigsaw puzzle are beginning to fit together,' declared Supt Lewis. Sadly, as time went on, it became apparent that a few of the pieces were missing.

Young's Wood was outside the parameters of the police search, although they had searched ditches and hedgerows in the area. But even if they had searched the wood would they have found Anne? If the 'deep freeze' theory was right, it is almost certain that she was not there when the searches were made. Evidence was given at the inquest by a gamekeeper who walked the woods regularly, with his dogs. The body was found in a clearing and was easily visible, yet neither he nor his dogs had noticed it. Nor, for that matter, had any poachers, many of whom would have been at large in the woods throughout that January. Not that poachers could be relied upon to admit being in the woods, but surely they would have come forward if they had found Anne.

Although Rose Grove Lane was used by courting couples in parked motor vehicles, none ever drove along the muddy cart-track for any great distance, and there were no signs of any vehicle anywhere near the place where Anne's body was found. Anne weighed eleven and a half stones, so if her body was later taken to the woods she must have been carried for a considerable distance by a very strong man, or two or more people. There were no signs of a vehicle's wheel-marks or dragging.

On the day of Anne's funeral, St Helen's Church, Wheathampstead, was full and many people who had come to pay their respects had to remain outside. Business premises closed so that staff could attend the service. When the church clock struck three the funeral was over, but the job of detecting the murder of 17-year-old Anne Noblett wasn't.

As soon as the 'deep freeze' theory was seen to account for Anne's freezing body, police wasted no time in checking deep freezer equipment within a 30-mile radius of Whitwell. These included poultry and meat storage sites, as well as owners of deep freeze vehicles, everything from ice cream vans to vehicles carrying frozen food. They established that there were scores of such vehicles buzzing around the Hertfordshire lanes, packed with meat, vegetables, poultry and fish. They cast their net far and wide, to London and throughout the Home Counties. A company executive told police, 'Really low temperatures can be achieved merely by plugging in a cable from a van to an electric point,' and said that drivers would normally unload unsupervised. It would be possible, he said, for a body to be carried about in such a

RIGHT From The Watford Observer

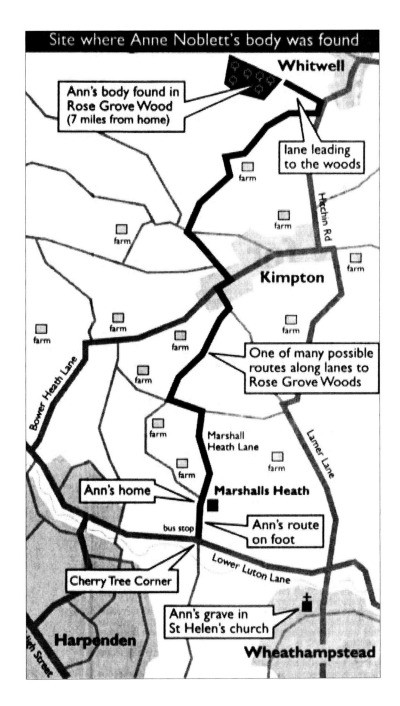

vehicle for weeks at a time, or even kept frozen in a bed, by inserting sticks of dry carbon dioxide of the type used to keep ice cream frozen in boxes, and pulling the bedclothes over to prevent gas escaping.

Police now concentrated on interviewing over 2,000 people. There were the usual house to house enquiries of local residents, in particular at Marshalls Heath and Whitwell. Had anyone seen a strange car in the area? Had anyone been in the woods? Had anyone seen any suspicious characters? There was a theory that whoever abducted Anne and later took her to the woods knew the area, so could be local. One man reported seeing a black Austin car parked in the road some distance from the wood, about a week before Anne was found. The man had to drive on to the grass verge to pass, and noticed that the letters on the number plate identified it as a Hertfordshire registration – RUR. He did not recall the remainder of the number, but noticed a well-built man sitting in the car. He was not traced.

In another report, a woman said she had noticed a young couple standing together at Church Green, Harpenden, about 5.45 p.m. She thought the girl fitted Anne's description. The woman asked directions to a doctor's surgery, and the girl said she knew where it was and the couple walked part of the way with the woman. If this was Anne, then who was the man she was with, and did they travel on the bus? Was he her killer?

The 'deep freeze' theory, however unusual – or unlikely – is a possibility. If it is correct, then Anne's killer, or killers, having murdered her soon after abducting her and re-dressing her, must have kept her body secretly frozen somewhere for up to about a month, and then driven her to the vicinity of Young's Wood, then carried her into the woods and placed her on the ground where she was found. If so, they were taking quite a risk. Why not dispose of the body when the murder occurred? Why not drive her miles away that very night to do so? The pathologist had given his opinion: he thought she had been kept in frozen conditions and the police acted accordingly. But pathologists can be mistaken.

One must look at the geography of the area. Anne was abducted in Marshalls Heath Lane, apparently when walking in a northerly direction towards her home. If forced into a vehicle travelling in the same direction, it would have been natural to continue up the lane, after which other quiet lanes lead naturally to Whitwell. On that quiet December evening it would have taken minutes to drive to the cart track, as courting couples did, where Anne could have been made to walk to the woods ahead. A local person would have known the way.

To establish how long Anne had lain where she was found, the police called in botanists from Rothamstead Experimental Station, Harpenden, to analyse the state of leaves and leaf mould found underneath her body. Crucially, the botanists' tests threw up what were deemed to be 'confusing results', when they suggested there was at least two weeks' difference in the growth of snowdrops and ferns underneath Anne's body and those around it, implying she had lain there for at least a fortnight undetected. But *were* these results 'confusing'? Or was it the case that they did not fit the 'deep freeze' theory? Did the police keep an open mind, rather than coming to one conclusion to the exclusion of any other? In short, was Anne forced to walk into the woods on the night of her abduction, and had she been murdered there and had she lain there since?

Said Detective Superintendent Elwell of Anne's killer: 'He may think he has committed the perfect crime, but we shall never rest until he is caught.' Until he is, the macabre chain of events surrounding the death of Anne Noblett will forever remain a mystery. But, having regards to Supt Elwell's words, are the police still looking?

The Verdict

It is easy to look back half a century and analyse a situation from one's armchair, and then pass judgement. Which is not to say that judgement will be correct. The question is: after she was murdered, was Anne Noblett's body really frozen and kept somewhere, then deposited in that wood? Even if investigating detectives had doubts about the veracity of the pathologist's conclusion, they would have considered this line of enquiry reasonable. What would be the point of employing an expert whose opinion, when given, is ignored?

In any case, what other options had the enquiry team? They interviewed over 2,000 people, sought and located such witnesses as they could to trace any suspect person or vehicle, appealed to the press, visited their peers in Essex who had a murder of their own, apparently unconnected as it happened. They brought in botanists, whose opinion was that Anne's body had lain *in situ* for at least a fortnight. It might have been more, who can say? It was a mild winter, but December nights can be cold nonetheless. Cold enough to freeze a corpse, left lying on the ground long enough. Applying a 'copper's nose', detectives might have had one or two suspects. If so, they were ruled out, presumably.

No person was arrested and charged with this crime. Could the person, or persons, who murdered Anne Noblett still be alive and, if so, have they been haunted these past years with what they did to an innocent young woman? Would it be too late to ask them to clear their conscience, and answer the questions Anne's family deserve to have answered?

Brookmans Park 1986

"Rape is a natural thing for a man to do"

It is a statistical fact that rape is almost always committed by men who know their victims, whether through long-term or short-term acquaintance. 'Stranger rape', the attack on the woman alone, is rare. This statistical fact is important to bear in mind when reading about John Francis Duffy and David Mulcahy, who were convicted of two murders and multiple rapes committed in the 1980s. Their crimes encompassed a wide area involving no less than four police forces: the Metropolitan Police, the British Transport Police, Surrey and Hertfordshire.

On 18th May, 1986, almost 30 years after the mysterious disappearance and murder of Anne Noblett, Hertfordshire was the focus of another, apparently similar, investigation that took on national significance, when a 29-year-old woman, Anne Lock, disappeared without trace. She was a secretary who worked at London Weekend Television, and lived with her husband in their fashionable home at Brookmans Park. That day, a Sunday, she left work about 8.15 p.m. and duly arrived at Brookmans Park station, near Hatfield, around ten o'clock, where she collected her bicycle which she had left there earlier. She never reached her home, only a short distance away, although her bicycle was found soon afterwards, still padlocked, on waste land not far away.

Anne Lock had been married only four weeks, and this, together with the discovery of her abandoned bicycle, made it very unlikely that she had somehow decided to simply vanish of her own accord. The fears of her family were realised when her decomposing body was discovered by railway workers on 21st July amid undergrowth on the railway embankment, just out of the parameters police had set for their search. Her hands were tied behind her back. Although it was impossible to tell whether or not she had been sexually assaulted, she almost certainly was.

It wasn't long before the police were linking her abduction and murder with two others, committed by the so-called railway killer, or killers, who police believed responsible for similar crimes. The first, on 29th December, 1985, was that of Alison Day, a 19-year-old student, who was murdered as she stepped from a train at Hackney Wick, east London. Seventeen days later police found her body in a canal. Her abductors had tied her hands behind her back, raped her, then garrotted her with a tourniquet. The second, on 17th April, 1986, was of Maartje Tamboezer, a 15-year-old Dutch schoolgirl, who was abducted and murdered at East Horsley, Surrey, as she cycled along a track near the railway. She was on her way to buy sweets before going on holiday the following day. She was found by two men the day after her disappearance. She too had been bound, raped, then strangled with a tourniquet.

The three murders had at least two things in common: all of the victims had been abducted for the purpose of rape, and probably killed to prevent possible identification of the killer; and they all took place at or near a railway. The bodies of Alison Day and Anne Lock yielded little in the way of scientific evidence, the former having lain in water, the latter being too decomposed. But although the killers had set fire to the body of Maarte Tamboezer, there were traces of semen and a small footprint nearby. The semen identified her attacker as a blood group A secretor, one in three of the male population.

In fact, there were two railway killers. Their gruesome catalogue of crime began in 1982, when two men raped a woman near Hampstead railway station, with at least a further eighteen women being raped the following year, all or most near railway stations. When three more women were raped in 1985, police set up Operation Hart, a computer database which logged details of 5,000 sex offenders and men with a history of violence against women. One of these was John Duffy, a 27-year-old carpenter who lived in Kilburn. He was 5 feet 4 inches tall and wore size four shoes. He had worked in the furniture department at Euston station, a job that meant travelling extensively on the railway. In 1985, after he became unemployed, he raped his estranged wife when she called at the Kilburn flat. On that occasion he gave a blood sample, which showed him to be of blood group A secretor. He appeared on the Operation Hart database. He was in the frame. But so were thousands of others.

On one of Duffy's court appearances, a detective took a rape victim to court and asked her if she recognised him. She did not, but Duffy recognised her. It is thought that for this reason Duffy decided that to allow future victims to live was too dangerous, and only four weeks later he murdered Alison Day. Duffy became a police suspect, especially when his blood group matched that of Maartje Tamboezer's killer. When police visited his flat in Kilburn they found a ball of 'paper string', which matched that found on his victims, and fibres found on his clothing matched some of those found on Alison Day's sheepskin coat. He was charged with murdering Alison Day, Maartje Tambooezer and Anne Lock, and seven counts of rape.

In February, 1988, John Duffy stood trial at the Old Bailey. During the trial, the judge ordered that the charge of murdering Anne Lock was to be withdrawn. He said, 'As a matter of law there is not sufficient evidence to bring in a verdict of guilty in respect of this matter... there is no direct evidence linking the killing with this defendant.' Duffy was convicted of the murders of Alison Day and Maartje Tamboezer, along with five rapes, and sentenced to life imprisonment with the recommendation that he serve at least thirty years. Although not convicted of the murder of Anne Lock, this investigation was nevertheless considered closed.

But the case was not over, at least as far as the other offences were concerned. Twelve years later, after John Duffy told a prison psychiatrist about his part in these dreadful crimes, the police launched a new investigation. Duffy had named an accomplice, David Mulcahy, a former school friend, whom police had also arrested,

Anne Lock

separately, on the first investigation. Then, they had no evidence to connect him. Now they did. Mulcahy, a plasterer, was arrested again, the evidence against him being Duffy himself, who would testify against him, and the new technology, DNA, which positively implicated Mulcahy with several of the rapes – as well as Duffy himself. Duffy was convicted of seventeen further sexual offences and given a further twelve years. Mulcahy was convicted of the two murders, with Duffy, of Alison Day and Maartje Tamboezer, and six rapes. He was sentenced to three life sentences and 24 years' imprisonment, as well as a further 18 years for conspiracy. A catalogue of wicked crimes ended with the incarceration – for their natural lives, surely – of two monsters.

9

STOCKING PELHAM 1969–70

The Kidnap and Murder of Muriel McKay

When Mr Rupert Murdoch, newspaper entrepreneur and owner of the *News of the World*, went on holiday with his wife, Anna, in December, 1969, to spend Christmas in Australia, his chauffeur-driven Rolls Royce was put at the disposal of Mr Alick McKay, Vice Chairman of the company. Mr McKay, 60, lived with his wife Muriel, 56, in Arthur Road, Wimbledon, their grown-up family having fled the nest, as they say. But the privilege of having a Rolls Royce was to have tragic consequences, in a sequence of events which started at their Wimbledon home and ended up at a 17th-century farmhouse at Stocking Pelham, near Bishop's Stortford, the address of two West Indian brothers, Arthur and Nizamodeen Hosein.

On Monday, 29th December, Mrs McKay prepared dinner at home for herself and her husband. Mr McKay was driven home from work in the Rolls Royce, arriving about 7.45. He dismissed the chauffeur, and rang the doorbell, using a special code known to his wife. There was no reply. He then found that the security chain was not in place and that the door was not locked. Stepping inside, he discovered a number of other things: a billhook, a long, axe-like tool used for hedge trimming, that the disc on the telephone, bearing their ex-directory number, had been carefully removed, some tape and twine, and a copy of *The People* newspaper, which the family did not take. He also found one or two of the rooms in some disorder, with drawers left open and furniture out of place, and that his wife's jewellery, valued at £600, was missing, and her shoes and handbag were on the stairs. What he could not find was his wife.

One can barely imagine the feelings of Mr McKay as he paced the floor, calling out his wife's name, looking for a sign that might provide an explanation for her absence and the strange items he had discovered. When he found none he called the police. Their first reaction might have been to consider Mrs McKay had gone out unexpectedly, to help in someone else's family crisis, perhaps; or that she had had an accident of some kind, or had even left her husband. But Mrs McKay's Ford Capri car was in the garage, and there was the strange mess and the missing jewellery. After calling his family, there was nothing for Mr McKay to do but wait, hoping against hope that there was an explanation, that his wife would turn up or the police would find her. Alas, some five hours after finding her missing his worst fears were realised: his wife had been kidnapped,

The telephone call came at 1.15 a.m. the next morning. The caller was a man. 'This is the Mafia Group Three. We are from America. We tried to get Rupert Murdoch's wife. We could not get her, so we took yours. Have one million pounds by Wednesday night or we will kill her.' Mrs McKay was being held to ransom for a sum of money her husband could not possibly find, her abductors having followed the Rolls Royce and seized her in the belief she was Mrs Murdoch.

There were clues, even at this early stage. First, a neighbour had seen a dark-coloured Volvo car driving slowly near Wimbledon Common. As he overtook it he saw what he thought were two Arabs inside. At 6 p.m. another neighbour saw a dark saloon in the driveway of the McKays' house. And the telephone call made to Mr McKay had been overheard by Terence Underwood, a late-night telephone operator. He had heard raised voices on the line, as well as the ransom demand. Just as significant was that Mr Underwood had been asked by the caller to connect him to the McKay household, implying that the caller did not know the number.

As for the claim that Mrs McKay was being held by the Mafia, the

Muriel McKay

police may have regarded this as either serious or, more likely, doubtful, and that it was a scare tactic designed to reinforce the kidnappers' demand. As with all kidnapping cases followed by a ransom demand, it was now a waiting game. In the meantime, the McKays' son, Ian, and his wife arrived from Australia, after which came another telephone call saying a letter would be arriving from Mrs McKay. So it did, the following morning, New Year's Eve. The letter, posted in Tottenham, read, 'Alick Darling, I am blindfolded and cold. Only blankets. Please do something to get me home. Please co-operate or I can't keep going. Muriel'.

The next day the letter was published in the national newspapers. The decision to do this was made by Mr McKay, himself a newspaper man, and his son-in-law. They held a press conference, inviting the kidnappers to contact them with 'instructions' on how to pay the ransom. They said he, Mr McKay, was ill with a bad heart, and that Mrs McKay needed treatment for arthritis, implying that an early settlement was necessary and hoping the ransom demand would be lowered as a result. This was the beginning of a cat-and-mouse game that would end up in the country lanes of east Hertfordshire, and ultimately at Stocking Pelham.

Eight days passed with no contact. What must the McKay family have gone through in that time? What must Mrs McKay herself have gone through – if she was still alive? It was bad enough that she was probably being kept in cold, dark conditions; but that she had been kidnapped in the mistaken belief that she was someone else would have undoubtedly angered and frustrated her kidnappers who may have killed her out of spite or frustration. When the contact came, by letter to the *News of the World*, it was to say Mrs McKay was receiving medical treatment, and that negotiations would continue 'once the police were out of the house'. The fact that there had been publicity, and that the police were obviously involved, was a dangerous tactic. In the kidnappers' minds it would put at risk the chances of successfully being paid the ransom, and enhanced the chances of detection, both factors being likely to frighten them off – but not, perhaps, until they had murdered Mrs McKay.

A series of telephone calls to the McKay household followed, but at no time was Mr McKay or any family member permitted to speak to Mrs McKay, neither was there any proof that she was still alive. Mr McKay insisted he could not pay a million pounds, but he was told to find it. He offered £20,000 as a first payment. He was told, 'That's not enough. It's up to you to get the money. It must be half a million,

first delivery.' On 21st January the McKay family was told they would receive two letters from Mrs McKay the following day, which would prove she was still alive. In fact, one letter arrived from Muriel. She wrote, 'I am deteriorating in health and spirit. Please keep the police out of this'.

Mr McKay demanded proof that his wife was still alive, and two further letters arrived. One contained fragments of Mrs McKay's coat and two-piece suit, and a piece of leather from one of her shoes. She had written, 'If only I could be home... I can't believe this has happened to me... it seems hopeless... you betrayed me by going to the police... you don't seem to be helping me... I beg of you to co-operate'. Both letters had been posted at Wood Green, but when were they written? There was no means of knowing. There was also a note from the kidnappers, saying that Mrs McKay would be executed on 2nd February unless a 'business date' for 1st February was kept. In fact, as later events would prove, it was almost certain that by now Muriel McKay had been murdered, and her abductors were focusing solely on obtaining the ransom in the knowledge that if it was paid she could never return to her desperate family.

Arrangements were made for the Rolls Royce, driven by the chauffeur and containing Ian McKay, to rendezvous with the kidnappers on 1st February, at a telephone kiosk in Tottenham. Half of the ransom sum, £500,000, was to be brought in a suitcase. This was arranged, except that two detectives would take the part of the chauffeur and Ian McKay, and the banknotes would be fakes, specially printed by the Bank of England, with a genuine £5 note on the top of each bundle. The Rolls Royce would be kept under police surveillance. At 10 p.m., as instructed, they proceeded to the telephone kiosk, where the telephone rang. 'Who is speaking?' asked the caller. 'Ian McKay,' said the detective, who was instructed to proceed to another kiosk. 'An error will be fatal,' said the caller. At the second kiosk they waited for 40 minutes, and when the telephone rang the undercover detective was told to look on the floor for a cigarette packet with further instructions. They were written on an empty packet of Piccadilly cigarettes. Now they were to proceed up the A10 to High Cross, Hertfordshire, where at the signpost for Dane End he would find two paper flowers marking the place to leave the suitcase.

At midnight, he found the flowers and left the suitcase. On that cold February night the two detectives waited in the Rolls Royce. But they weren't the only policemen waiting. Apart from the car that followed them, there were others, no doubt placed at strategic locations, and someone keeping an eye on the suitcase, presumably. A dark coloured Volvo turned up, driving towards the spot where the suitcase lay. It was noted that one of its rear lights was not working, but they were unable to get the number. The Volvo did not stop, but drove off into the night. At 2.20 a.m. the suitcase was recovered. It was back to the drawing board.

M3 – the kidnappers – telephoned the McKay household again. The caller said, 'We saw the cars parked all around. Did you know they were all policemen?' The caller went on, 'I am going to plead for your mum. I am fond of her, because she reminds me of my mum, you see.' They were playing mind games now, with the distraught family of Mrs McKay. You might think that the kidnappers, having turned up at the scene of the drop and found police waiting, might not have risked such a strategy again. But the police and kidnappers had different agendas: the police wanted to capture someone picking up the ransom, getting them 'bang to rights', whilst the kidnappers were motivated by greed. Another arrangement, by telephone, was made to hand over the money for the release of Mrs McKay.

This time, Alick McKay was instructed that he and his daughter, Diane, were to proceed to a telephone kiosk at Edmonton at 4 p.m. on Friday, 6th February. They were to have the money in two small suitcases. A different detective took the roll of Alick McKay, and a woman officer that of Diane, wearing Diane's pink coat to fool the kidnappers. The Rolls Royce would not be followed, but an armed detective was secreted in the boot. At the telephone kiosk they were instructed to go to another kiosk in Bethnal Green, and then to drive to Theydon Bois, then take the Underground to Epping, but not before the caller warned, 'If the police are about this time we will execute Muriel.' At Epping they were told to take a taxi to Bishop's Stortford, and leave the suitcases in the hedge opposite a Mini car at Gates Used Cars. The detective playing the role of Mr McKay, asked, 'Where is my wife?' He was told that Mrs McKay would telephone him at that kiosk once the suitcases had been dropped. 'Trust us,' he was told.

The police ordered a hire-car to take them to Bishop's Stortford. The armed officer who had hidden in the boot of the Rolls Royce lay on the floor of the hire-car, and at Gates Used Cars he crawled out and through the snow and hid in someone's garden. The suitcases were placed in the hedge, near the Mini. Two further armed officers waited, watching the suitcases. A Control Vehicle was parked up a mile away and a helicopter with more armed police stood by ready for take-off. The trap was set. It would be the last chance to capture the kidnappers.

Just after nine o'clock a dark-coloured Volvo with one rear light not working pulled up near the suitcases. Its registered number was XGO 994G. It contained two men of West Indian appearance. The driver leaned out, but drove off suddenly when a car behind hooted. The Volvo returned, four more times, but neither of its occupants got out to pick up the suitcases. As prosecution counsel would later say at the trial of two men arrested for the kidnapping, 'The Volvo was cruising around like a crow around its meat.' But where fear of capture made them hesitate, greed made them persist. Their hesitation proved fatal. The suitcases were spotted by two passers-by, one of whom stood guard over them while the other called the police. As the Volvo disappeared into the darkness, it was a policeman, not the kidnappers, who picked up the suitcases.

The suspects had fled and had not been identified. The ransom money had not been collected and Mrs McKay's whereabouts were still unknown. Police had found fingerprints on the letters and the empty cigarette packet, but they didn't know whose they were. But they did have something: the name and address of the registered owner of the Volvo. He was 33-year-old Arthur Hosein, who lived at Rooks Farm, Stocking Pelham, with his 21-year-old brother, Nizamodeen. The next morning the police were at the door.

Rooks farm comprised two 17th-century cottages knocked into one, situated on ten acres of land. It had been bought by Arthur Hosein two years previously. Evidently he kept pigs and a cow or two but little else. Neither of the Hoseins were farmers at all, in fact. Arthur was a tailor, or 'button finisher', by trade, and had moved to England

Police search Rooks Farm

from his native Trinidad in 1955. He was ambitious, and was in the habit of drinking whisky at his local pub, *The Raven*, Stocking Pelham. Nizamodeen, or Nizam, as he was known, arrived in England in 1969 on a visitor's permit and didn't go home. As well as arresting both men on suspicion of kidnapping Muriel McKay, the police searched Rooks Farm in search of evidence, not least for Mrs McKay herself, as well as the Volvo and anything else that would incriminate their suspects.

They searched everywhere. Every part of the house, every drain, every ditch, every nook and cranny. They searched ponds, and a policeman was lowered down a well to try and find Mrs McKay. They did not find her, nor a single shred of evidence that she had ever been there. They did find the Volvo, as well as a number of items connecting the Hoseins to the crime. There were paper flowers, similar to those marking the spot at High Cross where the first pickup was intended, an empty Piccadilly cigarette packet, similar to the one with the instructions in the telephone kiosk, a piece of paper, found in Nizam's trousers, bearing the number of the Mini marking the spot for the second pickup, sheets of blue paper, similar to the letters written by Mrs McKay and sent to her husband, sticking plaster similar to that found in the McKay household, presumably believed to have been used to gag Mrs McKay or maybe strap her wrists together. They also found a billhook in the kitchen. Arthur Hosein said he had borrowed it from a farmer friend because he wanted to 'chop up a calf', which Nizam said he had done and that he had fed it to the Hoseins' two Alsatian dogs. Some police officers were apparently able to identify Nazim as the driver of the Volvo on the second drop. Both brothers denied any knowledge of the crime.

Rumours abounded, particularly with regard to Mrs McKay's fate, notably that if she had been brought to the farm they could have got rid of her by chopping her up and feeding her to the pigs. Several farmers wrote to the police to say so. If true there would be no trace of her. Evidence would be given at the trial that Nizam Hosein had been seen chopping up a calf with the billhook found at the farm, and that he had fed it to the pigs. 'It was a woman, not a calf,' suggested the prosecution.

There was more incriminating evidence. As Nizam would admit at the trial, on 19th December he applied to the Greater London Council for details of the owner of the Rolls Royce car belonging to Mr Murdoch. He also admitted that it was he who had placed two paper flowers by the roadside, at High Cross – not that he knew of the purpose, but that it was at his brother's bidding; that he had driven the Volvo on 6th February to Gates Used Cars, to look for two suitcases, that he drove the Volvo to *The Raven* public house the same evening, arriving at about 10 p.m., and that he returned to Gates Used Cars; and that it was his handwriting on the note about the Mini. These admissions were all made to offload responsibility on to his brother and away from himself. Arthur Hosein's palm print was found on a ransom note sent to the McKay household, and his thumb and finger impressions on an envelope containing one of Mrs McKay's letters. His fingerprints were also found on the copy of *The People* newspaper, found in the McKay's home.

The police had caught the kidnappers, but they had not found their victim. Nevertheless, on 10th February they were both charged with kidnapping and murdering Muriel McKay. As far as the murder was concerned, this was very unusual, since it is almost always the case that before someone is charged the victim's body has been found and subjected to a post mortem examination, the latter usually providing vital forensic evidence to prove the case. Without a body, this would be a difficult case to prove. Indeed, the prosecution would not only have to prove the Hosein brothers had murdered Mrs McKay, but that she had been murdered at all.

At the trial at the Old Bailey, in September, 1970, Sir Peter Rawlinson, QC, prosecuting, came straight to the point. He told the jury, 'Can you imagine the horror of a woman waiting for her husband to return home, and minutes later, gagged and trussed, she is then driven away in the darkness?' She must have been murdered, he said, and there was no doubt that she had been kidnapped.

Arthur's Hosein's counsel said his client 'had nothing to do with the crime'. He maintained he had been at Rooks Farm on the day of the kidnap, and had gone out for a 'brief drive' in the afternoon. He had never heard of Muriel McKay. As he gave evidence, Arthur Hosein became more and more agitated and arrogant, and accused the police of beating him up. He said, 'It is hard to believe the wickedness, the vindictiveness and the cruelness of the police. I was co-operating in every way possible. I was treated very badly and tortured mentally and physically.' At one point he raised his hands, spread his fingers and said, 'These hands are artistic, not destructive. I am an artist, not a killer.' This, from a man who owned a pig farm. Nizam Hosein's defence was that he was bullied by his brother into doing the things he admitted, such as enquiring about the registered owner of the Rolls Royce, driving the Volvo, etc. He had never seen Mrs McKay at Rooks Farm and knew nothing of kidnap or murder.

Judge Sebag Shaw said that if either brother was innocent of kidnapping they must be innocent of murder. The jury took four hours to return Guilty verdicts on both accused. Of the kidnapping charge, the Judge said, 'Your conduct was cold blooded and

The Verdict

Kidnapping is a rare crime. Since its reason is usually to extort money against the threat of death to the victim, it is always a difficult crime for the police to tackle. Tackle it they must, in circumstances whereby if the victim is murdered they will be seen to have failed, even though it may not be their fault. They must tread a fine line. Do they simply cede to the kidnappers' demands and allow the money to be handed over in the hope the victim will be released unharmed? Or do they endeavour to capture them, and at the same time try to secure release of the hostage, with all the risks involved? It is their job to catch criminals, after all, and if they don't in one case there will be the chance someone else will be seized. They must also consider the victim's distraught family, as they weigh up whether to give in or go along with police tactics.

abominable. She was snatched from the security and comfort of her home and reduced to terror and despair.' Of the blackmail charges, he said, 'There could not be a worse case. You put Mrs McKay's family on the rack for weeks in attempts to extort money.' Both brothers were sentenced to life imprisonment, Arthur Hosein to serve at least 25 years, Nizamodeen Hosein 15. In November, 1970, Rooks Farm was sold by auction. Muriel McKay's body was never found.

I n this case, the police failed to secure the release of Muriel McKay. It is doubtful that it was possible to do so, no matter what they did. If the police had not been contacted, if the family had not gone to the media, if they had paid the ransom, Mrs McKay's safe release may have been secured. In the event, the police had to somehow feel the collar of at least one of the kidnappers as he picked up the suitcase. They were spotted, the kidnappers didn't collect and at some point they murdered Mrs McKay. At least the case was proved, though whether this was consolation to the McKay family is doubtful. What did Muriel McKay go through? We shall never know.

A s for Arthur and Nizamodeen Hosein, it is hard to imagine that Hertfordshire was ever home to such cruel, merciless men. They seized a middle-aged woman from her home, then tormented her family over a period of weeks, during which at some point they murdered her by means unknown and disposed of her body at a place unknown. At no point did they admit their crime, or offer a shred of remorse. They were sentenced to so-called 'life imprisonment', with recommendations to serve minimum sentences. But such people should never be released at all.

Hemel Hempstead 1990

"An offence of great gravity"

Over twenty years later Hertfordshire had another kidnapping case. When it came it bore stark resemblance to the abduction of Mrs McKay. Husband at work, wife at home; husband returns from work to discover his wife missing; the police are called, a ransom demand is made. This offence took place in February, 1990, and differed on three counts: it was committed by one person, the victim was rescued and the media, although informed, agreed to 'keep quiet', thus allowing police to conduct a delicate operation without outside pressures or interference. Due to the nature and the relatively recent commission of this offence, the names of the victim and her family have been omitted.

She was 49, the wife of a millionaire businessman. They had three children. She was at home, ironing, when a man burst through the door. It was about mid-day. He wore a boiler suit and a balaclava and was carrying a gun. He said he wanted money and forced her upstairs to get her purse, after which she was made to kneel on the floor with her hands behind her back. She was handcuffed, taken outside and forced into the boot of his car and driven off. She spent the night in the boot, alone and cold and in fear for her life. One can barely imagine her thoughts as she lay in the darkness for nineteen hours, before a bin liner was placed over her head and she was taken somewhere unknown. It was an upstairs room above a shop in Hemel Hempstead Old Town, where she was blindfolded and left with one hand handcuffed to a radiator and a bucket for her convenience. Her abductor told her he would be making contact with her husband and left, telling her she would be watched and not to cry out.

When her husband arrived home it was obvious something was amiss: the iron still switched on, his wife's car still in the garage, her purse

Old Town, Hemel Hempstead
The High Street

lying on the kitchen floor. He informed the police, who requested a media blackout. It wasn't until 12.15 p.m. the next day, a Friday, that the caller made a demand, saying '£100,000' or '£500,000'. With another call came a demand for £500,000, later reduced to £250,000. He used an electronic device to disguise his voice, which earned him the nickname, 'The Dalek'.

On the Monday the husband collected £250,000 from his bank, and that night The Dalek called again, telling him to go to Gaddesden Row where he would find a tape cassette in a box on a pile of concrete. On tape, in his Dalek voice, the kidnapper said his wife was being kept in conditions that were 'severely inhospitable', and then he heard her voice, on tape. She had eaten only two biscuits, she said, and added, 'I am sure you are doing all you can to help me. Keep your spirits up and I will try to do the same.'

The kidnapper's plans were then thwarted. On that Monday morning, his victim, still imprisoned above the shop premises, had heard the clanking bottles of a milk float and called out for rescue. Then, her cries were not heard. On Tuesday morning they were. The milkman heard her and called the police. What relief she must have felt when police officers forced their way into the room and cut her free. She was given medical attention and reunited with her husband and family. Her abductor, 43-year-old John Warrington, was arrested shortly afterwards when he turned up at the premises. A 'failed businessman', he had been desperate for money and had selected his victim carefully. As an aspiring author, he had based the kidnap on a novel he had written but had failed to have published. He failed with the real thing too. At St Albans Crown Court the Judge told him, 'What you have pleaded guilty to are offences of great gravity, because they strike at the roots of other people's lives and their ability to live peaceably without fear. It was no thanks to you that your victim was eventually freed. Rather it was through her courage, observation and clear-headedness. What you did hardly bears thinking about.'

What hardly bears thinking about is what Warrington might have done if his victim had not been rescued. Even if the ransom had been paid, could he have let her go? She had seen his car, she had seen him – though not his face – and heard his voice. In the event he was sentenced to 15 years imprisonment, reduced on appeal to 13 years. With remission he served just 4½ years, minimal punishment for such a crime whilst his victim would live with the scars forever.

10

Hoddesdon 1970

The 'Red Mini' Murder

That 20-year-old Nicola Brazier had everything to live for was not in doubt. One look at her picture says it all: attractive, vivacious, smiling and smartly dressed. She had just passed her driving test and bought a red Mini car, which she would use to drive from her place of employment at Aylesbury, Bucks, to keep a business appointment at Nazeing, in Essex, 35 miles away. But Nicola never arrived. For her journey, through what for her was unchartered territory, ended in her rape and murder. This shocking crime was 'detected' by the police, yet the killer would not stand trial. Nor would his name ever be published. Instead, he will forever be known as 'Mr X'.

Nicola lived at Whitchurch, near Aylesbury. She worked as a secretary for a promotions firm and this, her first 'business' trip, was an important one that might have earned a better position as a representative with the company. Alone in her Mini, she left Aylesbury sometime before noon on Wednesday, 16th September, 1970, for her 3 p.m. appointment at Nazeing. At 3.45 someone at the Nazeing firm telephoned to say she had not arrived. Nothing further was heard from Nicola: that maybe she had broken down, or got lost, or had taken ill. She was considered reliable and trustworthy, and had taken the appointment seriously. Where had she got to?

The first breakthrough came at 3.15 a.m. the following morning, when a policeman found her Mini unattended at Broxbourne railway station, just a mile and a half from her intended destination. The car

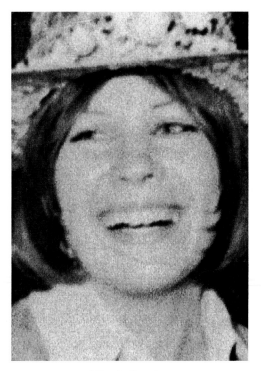

Nicola Brazier

was unlocked. In the parcel compartment of the driver's door were a pair of tights and knickers. They would later be identified as Nicola's. There was no sign of the ignition key, or any valuables. There was nothing to indicate where Nicola was, or why the car should be parked there. Nothing was heard from her or about her throughout that day, but that evening her family would have the answer they would have dreaded.

An Edmonton man with his wife and two children had visited the Woodman public house at Wormley West End, near Hoddesdon. They had their collie dog with them, and decided to go for a walk in nearby Bencroft Wood, a local beauty spot. There, in a clearing, the man saw what he thought was a tailor's dummy leaning against a tree. 'I thought it was a dummy because the skin was so white,' he said, and when he touched a leg with his foot he expected a 'hollow' noise. Instead, he realised it was a body. He and his family hurried back to the Woodman and called the police.

Detective Sergeant Gordon Smith attended the scene from Hoddesdon police station. He discovered that the dead woman, as it was, was fully clothed except for her underwear, and wore knee-length black leather boots, and that her hands were tied tightly at the wrists behind her back, with rope, or sash cord. The woman, identified as Nicola, had been shot through the head. The bullet had entered one side of her head and exited the other. It was never found. In that leaf-strewn wood its total disappearance is scarcely surprising. But a search did uncover a spent cartridge case of .32 calibre, marked 'H.P' (indicating Hirtenberger Patrone, an Austrian weapons manufacturing company). Nicola had been shot at close range with a semi-automatic weapon. The pathologist who attended estimated the time of death at about six or seven o'clock the previous evening.

When Nicola's body was examined in the mortuary at Hertford County Hospital it was found to have abrasions and bruises on the thighs, and there had been some 'internal bleeding', suggesting there had been 'forceful intercourse'. Semen was found inside the vagina. Nicola's bra had been undone and was pulled up over her breasts. She was alive and tied up when intercourse took place. The pathologist was unable to categorically say she had not 'consented'. Held at gunpoint, her wrists tightly bound, sustaining cuts and bruises: there would hardly have been 'consent'. Nicola had been abducted and taken to the woods where she had been forced to remove her tights and knickers, but allowed to put on her boots, then tied up and raped and murdered in cold blood. There can be little doubt that it was her killer who drove her Mini to Broxbourne railway station, although why was never firmly established. Maybe his own car was parked thereabouts.

A small amount of money had been stolen from Nicola's handbag and, significantly, three cheques from her chequebook. But what the police desperately wanted to find was the bullet that killed Nicola, and the gun that fired it. After six days of searching they found neither in the woods, although they had recovered the spent cartridge case. Nicola's car having been found abandoned at Broxbourne railway station, they considered the possibility that her killer had taken a train, and frogmen searched the New River in the hope of finding the gun. There was no trace of it. Several people came forward to say they thought they had seen Nicola's Mini, registration number 880 TE, being driven by a woman. One 'sighting' had her driving along the A414, about 1 p.m., in good time for her appointment. It seems she may have become confused in Hoddesdon, then driven over Dobbs Weir towards Nazeing, where she was sighted driving along Water Lane. It was here, at the junction with Epping Road, that the police thought she met her killer, a man who was seen to get into a Mini, after which no further sightings were established. We may speculate here that Nicola stopped to ask directions, that the man whom she was unfortunate enough to encounter was armed and abducted her.

Appealing for witnesses, the police distributed thousands of 'Have you seen this girl?' leaflets, and the following Wednesday they 'reconstructed' events, when a policeman's wife, who resembled Nicola and wore similar clothes for the occasion, drove Nicola's Mini along the route detectives believed she had driven. Police visited houses near Bencroft Wood and asked residents 'if they had heard a shot'. They had, but as one explained, 'We get a lot of shooting in the wood and take no notice.' They established that on the evening of the murder a member of the pop group, Pink Floyd, had moved into the area. He and members of the group were seen and eliminated, but even so police considered one of their 'hangers on' could have been the stranger who apparently got into Nicola's car. They did everything possible, and maybe more, whilst they could not know that just three days after the crime Nicola's killer was already dead.

RIGHT **"Have you seen this girl?"**
Police poster showing Nicola and her Mini

MURDER
BENCROFT WOODS, HODDESDON.

HAVE YOU SEEN
THIS GIRL?

20 YEARS,
5'2'',
GOOD FIGURE,
GREY EYES,
HIGH CHEEK BONES,
ATTRACTIVE FEATURES,
MID-BROWN HAIR WITH AN
AUBURN TINGE.

DRESSED:
IN A LIGHT TAN SUEDE
ZIP-FRONTED WAISTCOAT
AND MATCHING MINI SKIRT,
BLACK LONG SLEEVED POLO
NECK SWEATER AND
BLACK KNEE LENGTH BOOTS.

OR THIS CAR
RED MORRIS MINI 880 T.E.
WITH A GREEN STICK-ON SUN VISOR

BELIEVED MURDERED DURING EVENING OF WEDNESDAY 16th. SEPTEMBER, 1970.
HER CAR WAS FOUND AT BROXBOURNE RAILWAY STATION ON THURSDAY 17th. SEPTEMBER, 1970.

ANY INFORMATION CONTACT HODDESDON 68444 OR NEAREST POLICE STATION.

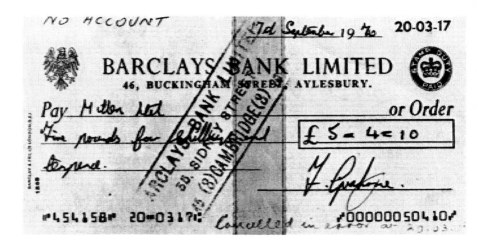

Stolen cheque
Fraudulently signed in the name 'F. Grahame', the cheque was used to purchase
records in a store in Cambridge

There were two significant developments after the crime: one, the
following day, the other over two months later.

The first took place on the morning of Thursday, 17th September,
when a man went to a music shop in Cambridge and bought two
records. To pay for the purchase he presented a cheque, drawn on
Barclays Bank, Ltd, Aylesbury, and signed 'F. Grahame'. A Cambridge-
shire address was written on the beck of the cheque. Cheques in those
days were not 'personalised', bearing the payee's name, in print. The
cheque was one of those stolen from Nicola's chequebook, and the
name and address were false. It seems there was no reliable description
of the man, which may be understandable in a busy city centre store.

The second development concerned a holdall, which was found
in a left luggage locker at Euston Station. It was taken from the left
luggage box in September, and held for two months at the Found
Property Office without the contents being checked, which was normal
procedure. On 26th November, when the contents were checked,
the holdall was found to contain Nicola's driving licence, RAC

membership card, a wallet-notepad, and the chequebook, showing two outstanding cheques, and a petrol receipt issued at Harpenden on the day she disappeared, 16th September. Also in the holdall was a Browning semi-automatic pistol, .32 calibre and 17 H.P. rounds of ammunition, four still in the magazine, the remainder contained in a matchbox. There was also a modified leather gun holster. Police wasted no time in trying to trace the history of the holdall, discovering that one such was purchased by a man on 19th September at a 'hitch-hiker' shop near Euston station. Enquiries were made to trace the manufacturer of the holster, but this line of enquiry became somewhat academic due to the astonishing success detectives had with their enquiries regarding the pistol.

Its case history is long and complicated. Suffice to say it was manufactured in Belgium and sent to the UK in 1917. In 1950 it was purchased as part of a 'bulk buy' by the Ministry of Supply, and sold in 1952 to a firearms dealer, and then sold again to another firearms dealer. From there, the police investigation into its history switched to Canada, after which they lost track of it until they established the name of a man in Sussex who owned it 1956. In 1960 he moved to Zambia, and in 1968 to South Africa when he sold it to an arms dealer who sold it to a British seaman. In 1969 it was sold again, and ended up back in the UK, when it was sold to a North London man who gave it, along with eighteen rounds of ammunition, to a man later identified as 'Mr X' to pay off a debt. The next thing that was known about it was its appearance in the left luggage box at Euston station. It was, without doubt, the weapon used to kill Nicola Brazier. Significantly, there was a fingerprint on the gun. All the police had to do was identify whose it was.

All they had to do, indeed! First, they needed a fingerprint to compare with the one on the pistol. In those pre-computerised days it would be no easy task to search records − if he was on record (and if it was a 'he'). The only way was to examine the records was one by one, thousands, millions maybe, of fingerprints. Where should they start? Hertfordshire? Greater London? South-East England? Men between, say, 20 and 40 years of age? In fact, the police already had a fingerprint for comparison, and they had had it since 20th September, just four days after the murder. Which is not to suggest anyone could possibly had known.

On 19th September, Mr X, as we know him, was found dead on the railway at Potters Bar. His body was taken to Barnet hospital where it was routinely fingerprinted. At first, police had no cause to believe he was Nicola's killer, but in January they did. Detective Chief Inspector Chaffe of Scotland Yard had 22 years of fingerprints experience. He compared the prints of Mr X with those on the cheque fraudulently presented at Cambridge, and those on the property recovered from the left luggage box: the petrol receipt, the notepad and the pistol — the murder weapon. They were all made by the same person, Mr X.

Mr X was a married man who lived with his wife and one child at Cheshunt. He was self employed, with the use of two vehicles in the course of his employment. One was a Jaguar saloon. Police examined it and discovered that the radio compartment had a space 'big enough to take a gun and holster'. They also examined a Bedford Dormobile van, previously owned by Mr X and only recently sold. The vehicle had a compartment above the front offside wheel containing a piece of rope, or sash cord, similar to that used to tie Nicola's wrists. Mr X had driven the Jaguar on the day of the crime.

The inquest into the death of Nicola Brazier was held at Hertford in April, 1971. The Coroner was Mr J.D. Bolton. The jury duly heard that there was no doubt that the fingerprints were those of Mr X, and that the Browning pistol had killed Nicola. There was no powder on Nicola's hands to suggest she had fired the gun (there might have been a suggestion her hands had been bound afterwards, however unlikely); nor could the gun have been fired accidentally. 'It is an extremely safe weapon. It cannot be fired accidentally,' ballistics expert John McCafferty told the jury, adding that the gun and spent cartridge recovered at the scene 'matched exactly'.

Today, DNA would have conclusively confirmed or otherwise, that a named suspect had had intercourse with Nicola, in circumstances here amounting to rape. This technology was not available in 1970, but there was evidence of blood. Bloodstains found on Nicola's skirt were her own, blood group 'AB'. The semen, and seminal stains on her skirt, had secretions of blood group 'O', found in about one in three of the population. So, whilst this alone did not conclusively rule Mr X in, neither did it rule him out.

Detective Chief Superintendent Ron Harvey was the officer in charge of the police investigation. He told the court that Nicola had never been known to pick up strange men. She had once told a friend that her attitude to sexual danger was that if a man was determined to rape it was futile to resist and get hurt, that it was better to submit and seek medical attention afterwards. Nicola, he said, was a proud and ambitious girl who had been given a chance to prove herself (at work). 'Practically nothing would have prevented her from keeping that appointment.' Of Mr X, DCS Harvey said, 'It seems that with the gun he gained strength.' It was his belief, he said, that because of this his behaviour had become out of keeping with his normal character.

Mr X was dead; he could not stand trial. The evidence against him was strong, but circumstantial. DCS Harvey spoke of the main points: that he had been given the murder weapon as payment of a debt and that he was the last known person to have it in his hands; that his fingerprints were on the weapon, and the cheque, taken from Nicola when she was killed and passed the following day in a shop in Cambridge; there were eighteen rounds of ammunition sold to Mr X when he bought the gun, and when it was found in the left luggage box there were 17, the missing one (a cartridge case) being found at the scene of the crime; the rope, or sash cord, used to tie Nicola's wrists, was similar to that found in the Bedford van, recently owned by Mr X, and was essential in his employment. 'There is one man whom I would have charged with murder, but he is now dead,' said DCS Harvey. He also said that the handwriting on the cheque had been 'proven' by an

Police and coroner refuse to identify red mini murder suspect

NICOLA'S KILLER UNNAMED 'MR X'

The Verdict

R ape and murder are the wickedest of crimes. But, again, let it be said, they are rare crimes, almost always committed in circumstances where offender and victim are acquainted, however tenuously. The attack by the stranger is unlikely, anywhere. Words of assurance, one hopes, for the readers of these pages, and in particular this chapter.

R arer still, unheard of perhaps, is a case where a jury returns a verdict of guilty, yet the name of the offender is not released to the public in such a serious case. At the inquest into Nicola Brazier's murder, Mr R. Lee, representing the police, said, 'We have decided that it is improper for us to reveal this man's name, either now or at a future date, because no usefulness would be obtained, and a

expert to be that of Mr X. Whether this would have stood up under cross examination at a trial is doubtful, but this is a matter which need not be dwelt upon.

The inquest jury took fifteen minutes to return a verdict of 'Murder by Mr X'. The Coroner then declared he would not be named: it would not serve the 'public interest', it would 'harm his relatives and friends'. He commended all police officers 'involved in these long and difficult investigations'. As for Mr X, one wonders about his state of mind. Having set out armed, he committed the most outrageous crimes upon a young woman, and then the very next day calmly and fraudulently obtained property, a couple of records, by passing a stolen cheque. And yet, just two days after that, he took his life on the railway. Why? Out of remorse? Fear of capture and imprisonment? The shame that would have befallen him and his family? We will

---

great deal of harm would be done to his relatives and associates.' He was supported by the Coroner. 'I intend not to invade further the privacy to which any individual in this country is entitled. I hope the matter may now be allowed to rest there.' One can see that it would be hard on the man's family and friends, who were, after all, innocent of any crime. It was obviously a considered decision.

But it was the wrong decision, for it left loose ends flapping in the breeze of rumour. The public knew the man who killed Nicola Brazier was dead just days after her murder. There would be other dead men in the hospital then too, and elsewhere; some of their names would have been known, names that could be brought into the frame of suspicion as people wondered who the killer was. What about the families of those men? Mr X's name should have been published — at that time. But now, a generation on, it is best left as 'Mr X'.

never know. Lastly, one cannot help but reflect on this tragic case: a young woman going about her lawful business, lost in a strange town, abducted at gunpoint and made to drive to lonely woodland where she is tied up and raped, then shot and left where she lay, without even the dignity of wearing her underwear. What she would have gone through. There are no words.

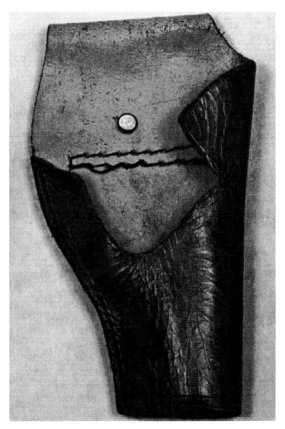

The modified leather gun holster,
found in a left luggage locker at Euston railway station

The Bovingdon Bug

Graham Young,
the Bovingdon Poisoner, 1971

Management and staff at Hadlands were mystified – and very worried. With two of their workforce dead in the past five months, and others stuck down by what had become known as the 'Bovingdon Bug', there had been a full medical enquiry into working conditions at the Bovingdon plant that manufactured photographic instruments. To assure workers that the chemicals they handled were safe, the management held a meeting with the entire workforce in the canteen.

That June, Bob Egle, aged 60, had taken ill. He was Chief Storeman at Hadlands, and had worked alongside Fred Biggs and Ronald Hewitt. And, since 10th May, a new chap, 24-year-old Graham Young. Mr Egle had never suffered any serious illness, yet on 1st June he came home from work complaining of sickness and diarrhoea. He was off-colour until he and his wife went on holiday to Great Yarmouth, after which he appeared to recover, returning to work on 28th June.

The next day Mr Egle was sick again, complaining of numbness at his fingertips and soreness when he combed his hair. He found he could not walk properly and was unable to sleep for pain. He vomited black liquid and was admitted to hospital, suffering from such excruciating pain he threatened to jump out of a window and had to be restrained. When his condition worsened he was transferred to another hospital by which time his respiratory muscles had failed and he was unable to speak. He died on 7th July. A post mortem examination gave the cause of death as Bronchopneumonia and Guillain Barre Polyneuritis.

Mr Hewitt then took ill, suffering from severe stomach pains, vomiting and a burning sensation at the back of his throat. Shortly afterwards he left his employment at Hadlands, after which he quickly recovered. Towards the end of September it was the turn of Peter Buck, a works manager, and soon after that David Tilson, aged 26, a clerk, who both took ill. Mr Tilson's condition became worse. His G.P. diagnosed fibrositis. After a period of sick leave he returned to work, still suffering from pains in his legs, but his health deteriorated and he was admitted to hospital. His hair started to fall out, but on 28th October he was discharged. He was re-admitted on 1st November, by which time had lost one and a half stones in weight. The doctor who treated him remarked, 'Here was a man with a full beard and a mass of hair who came back into hospital like a three-quarters plucked chicken.'

In the meantime, on 15th October, Mr Jethro Batt, a contract wireman at Hadlands, had an unfortunate experience at work. He was working late, until 7 p.m. On some evenings he had give Graham Young a lift home to Hemel Hempstead, and that evening Young made Mr Batt a cup of coffee. Taking just one sip, he noticed it had a peculiar taste. He said so to Young who replied, 'What do you think I'm trying to do, poison you?' Three weeks later it was Mr Batt's turn to be admitted to hospital, suffering from violent stomach pains, pains in his chest and legs, loss of concentration, hallucinations and alopecia – loss of hair. His big toes were rigid and painful and there was excruciating pain in the soles of his feet. Later, he would tell police that he had seen himself in World War One trenches, in scenes with bayonets, and lying on a mortuary slab. He said that if he'd had a shotgun he would have killed himself. Thallium was detected in his urine.

After the death of Bob Egle, Mrs Diana Smart worked in the stores.

On 20th October she suffered a severe bout of sickness accompanied by stomach pains and had to go home. After seeming to recover she returned to work, but just two days later, at work, she was again taken ill. She was unable to return to work until December.

Frederick Biggs, 56, also sometimes worked in the stores. In early September he took ill with sickness and diarrhoea, but that month he went on holiday with his wife, and seemed to get better. On 26th October, at work, he again fell ill and had to take sick leave. The following weekend, Mr Biggs began to suffer severe pain in his toes, had difficulty in walking and suffered pains in the chest. On 4th November he was admitted to hospital. His condition deteriorated and he was transferred to the National Hospital for Nervous Diseases, by which time he was semi conscious. Polyneuritis was diagnosed, a trachectomy was performed and he was placed in a breathing machine. He died on 19th November.

In trying to account for the high sickness rate, management were worried that there might be contamination by thallium salts, used in the manufacture of lenses, as the firm made photographic equipment. But they bought their lenses ready-made; thallium salts were not used in the manufacturing process at Hadlands at all. The Factories Inspectorate carried out a full investigation, and concluded the cause of so many illnesses was probably a virus. Yet many of the symptoms of those who had taken ill were of poisoning by thallium or antimony. Which brings us back to the meeting, held at Hadland's premises, immediately after the death of Frederick Biggs.

A local G.P. addressed the workforce. He tried to assure them that there was no cause for panic, and that the viral cause of the 'Bovingdon Bug' would soon be identified. Dr Anderson, head of the investigation team, made himself available for questions. Neither he nor the management team could have expected the 24-year-old storekeeper, Graham Young, to ask, 'Do you not think, doctor, that the symptoms of the mysterious illness are consistent with thallium poisoning?'

It would have taken the learned doctor by surprise on two counts: one, that a young storekeeper would know anything at all about thallium; and two, that the young storekeeper was right. Not surprisingly, they decided to check out the man who, barely five months previously, about the time when the catalogue of sickness began, had applied for and been given a job at the factory. They telephoned the police, setting off a chain of events that would lead to the arrest of a cold and merciless killer. One call was enough for the police to uncover the damning fact that nine years before Graham Young had been convicted of poisoning three people, for which he had been sent to Broadmoor from where he had been released the year before.

In fact, in 1962 Graham Young was convicted of poisoning his father, sister and a school friend. None of his actions then proved fatal, but he was committed to Broadmoor Hospital by Justice Melford Stevenson who made a Restriction Order for fifteen years. Yet as early as 1970 there was talk of Young's release, which concerned his aunt and sister, so much so they discussed their apprehension with a consultant psychiatrist at the hospital. Nevertheless, Young was granted a period of home leave, to live with his sister in Hemel Hempstead. In February, 1971, he was released to attend a 13-week course in Industrial Storekeeping at a Government Training Centre in Slough. Neither the police in Hertfordshire nor management at Hadlands were made aware of these facts.

When Young applied for the job at Hadlands he informed the company that prior to his attendance at the Government Training Centre he had not previously been employed due to hospitalisation and convalescence. Hadlands then contacted the Centre, who sent them a copy of a report by Young's doctor. The report was on unheaded paper: after, all a prospective employer would hardly be expected to take on someone subject of a report with 'Broadmoor' written across the top of the page. It stated that Young had had a 'personality disorder', which had resulted in hospitalisation throughout his adolescence. It went on, 'He has made a full recovery and is entirely fit for discharge'.

There was no mention of him poisoning three people some years before.

By now Young was living in a bedsit at Maynard Road, Hemel Hempstead. When police called he was not there, but searching his room they found a phial of thallium and a foolscap diary, along with books and other documents on toxicology, death, the supernatural, pictures of Adolph Hitler and other Nazi paraphernalia. The next day Young was arrested at his father's house at Sheerness, Kent. He was brought to

Graham Young

Hemel Hempstead to be interviewed by senior detectives, led by Chief Superintendent Harvey. He admitted the diary and the entries therein were his. He said the contents were notes he had compiled for a novel he intended to write. He denied all responsibility for the deaths of Bob Egle and Frederick Biggs, and causing illness to others.

However, in a further interview, Young admitted administering thallium to four people at Hadlands: Messrs Egle and Biggs, both fatally, and Tilson and Batt. He expressed concern over Mr Batt's condition, and was able to tell the officers the doctor should treat him with Dimercaprol Potassium Chloride. He further admitted administering antimony potassium tartrate to Messrs Buck and Hewitt, and Mrs Smart, at Hadlands, and to Trevor Sparkes, whom he had met at the Government Training Centre, Slough. When shown his diary he admitted his victims were all identified therein by the initial of their Christian names. He declined to make a written statement, but was able to identify all of the chemicals found in his room. He said the phial of thallium the police had discovered was his 'exit dose', which he intended to take in the event of arrest. He had meant to have it on his person, but had left it in his bedsit by mistake.

On 22nd November a post mortem examination was carried out on Frederick Biggs. Samples were taken for toxicological analysis. Above normal concentration of thallium was found. Mr Biggs had been poisoned. Young was charged with his murder. He had nothing to say.

Thallium is a highly toxic, lead-like metal, similar to mercury. Its usage in industry has been in pesticides, notably rat poison. It is, or was, available in the form of salts, being soluble in water, colourless and tasteless. Human consumption of thallium causes hair loss, nerve pains in the joints and extremities, especially the big toes, and, as events proved on Young's hapless victims, excruciating pain so unbearable that the weight of bedclothes can be enough to make a victim cry out in pain. Young administered thallium acetate, knowing or believing the consequences would be fatal. He also administered antimony potassium tartrate, also soluble in water, to his remaining victims, knowing it was unlikely to be fatal but would make them ill, causing diarrhoea, vomiting, muscular weakness and convulsions. So how could a storekeeper acquire such dangerous substances?

Graham Young somehow got his hands on poison of some kind when he was on the Government Training Course, at Slough. With it, he poisoned Trevor Sparkes, who was also on the course, though not fatally. The poisons he used at Hadlands he first purchased from a pharmacist who worked at a chemist's shop at Wigmore Street, London. On that occasion he bought 25 grammes of antimony potassium tartrate, signing the register as 'Mr M.E. Evans', a fictitious

The mind of a killer

Some of Young's drawings were recovered from his bedsit

name he had used to obtain poisons prior to his conviction in 1962. On a second visit to the chemist's he acquired more antimony, and this time some thallium. Having acquired the poisons, he set about administering them. It all came down to cups of tea and coffee.

Hadlands were good employers, providing free mid-day meals and free beverages to all staff. Tea and coffee were served at 11 a.m. and 3 p.m., brewed in the kitchen and then taken around the premises, including to the stores, by a tea lady. After each tea break the tea lady locked the kitchen door, but usually unlocked it at 5.30 p.m. to allow employers working overtime to make their own tea and coffee.

Young made it his business to collect the afternoon tea at the stores entrance and take it to his workmates. These were Messrs Egle, Biggs, Hewitt and Tilson. Mr Egle was the first to take ill; as we have seen, he died in July. In his diary entry, Young referred to the danger of doctors noticing the similarities between Mr Tilson's symptoms and those of the now deceased Mr Egle. He wrote, 'It is quite likely that the similarities of the symptoms to those preceding the death of "B" (Egle) may have been recognised, and the death certificate subjected to closer scrutiny'. In another diary entry, he refers to an earlier 'lethal dose' of thallium, and this is thought to refer to the death of his stepmother in 1962. Later, he would admit poisoning her too, a murder for which he was never charged. Nor could he ever be, since his stepmother's ashes were scattered and could not therefore be examined.

Bob Egle was cremated too, but his ashes had been interned at St Mary's churchyard, at Gillingham, near Loddon, in Norfolk. One of the policemen who went to recover the casket containing the ashes was Detective Constable Brendan Hayden, now retired. Says Detective Sergeant Hayden, as he became: 'We visited the coroner to enquire what procedure had to be followed to exhume the ashes.' In fact, exhuming the ashes of a deceased person was hitherto unknown in

RIGHT **Ex-Detective Constable Brendan Hayden**

this country. They found the casket just two feet deep in the ground. Examination of the remains showed the presence of thallium. Young found himself charged with a second murder, and afterwards with two counts of attempted murder, by administering thallium to David Tilson and Jethro Batt, and four charges of administering antimony potassium tartrate to Messras Hewitt, Buck and Diana Smart, at Hadlands, and Trevor Sparkes, at the Government Training Centre, Slough.

Sparkes, in fact, was a fellow trainee on the Training Course. He and Young became friendly. He described Young as an 'intelligent man with an unusual knowledge of medicine'. He said Young grew a Hitler moustache and adopted Hitler's hairstyle. Sparkes drank some wine, after which he developed pains in the stomach and suffered from vomiting and pains in the testicles. The symptoms persisted, and Sparkes, discussing his illness with Young, was advised by the latter to take bromide. Later, having secured employment at Hadlands in May, and acquired thallium and antimony on 5th June, Young was well set to practise his evil campaign of poisoning on his colleagues.

Of thallium, Young wrote in his diary, 'My experience of the drug has been only of lethal doses which, in both instances, led to rapid deterioration and death'. He was referring at the time to the lethal dose to Mr Egle, and another to his stepmother in 1962. Mr Hewitt recalled Young being in the habit of stirring teas. David Tilson also took tea with Young, but because Young kept putting sugar in it he tended not to drink it. Nonetheless, after drinking tea he took ill at home, losing the feelings in his toes and suffering pains in his legs. Young clearly intended to kill him, as his diary entry shows: 'Had, as was intended, the full amount (of thallium) been ingested, the resultant illness would have had a fatal resolution within 7–10 days'. He went on to write that if Mr Tilson had been hospitalised he would have visited him and administered a fatal dose by giving him a miniature brandy. Clearly, his heartlessness knew no bounds.

Mr Tilson survived. So did Jethro Batt, of whom Young had

enquired, 'What do you think I'm trying to do, poison you?' Indeed he was. Young's diary: 'A second development, which I now regret, is that "J" has been afflicted. The administration was Friday night, and as only approximately one third of the dose was ingested it is difficult to say how severe the resultant illness will be'. Mr Batt consumed about 5 grains. That would have been fifteen grains if he had drank all of the coffee, a fatal dose. Later, Young wrote, 'I hope that he will soon recover'. Was this out of contrition, or because Mr Batt was his lift home after work?

Of Mrs Diana Smart, to whom Young administered antimony, he wrote, "D" irritated me intensely yesterday, so I packed her off with an attack of sickness. I gave her sufficient to shake her up, though I now regret I didn't give her a larger dose...'. He knew antimony was not the killer thallium was. Of administering thallium to Mr Frederick Biggs, Young wrote, ' "F", whom I grew to like, has been the most recent subject of my attentions. I have administered a fatal dose of the special compound and anticipate reports of his illness on Monday. He should die within the week'. Later he wrote, 'In the event of "F" 's death the last problem will be "J" ' and, providing that hurdle is passed the battle will be over. Too many health authorities are becoming involved...'. Again he wrote, 'It seems a shame to condemn such a likeable man to such a horrible end. He will decline in the next few days. It will be a merciful release for him, as if he remains alive he will be permanently impaired. It is better that he should die. It will remove one more casualty from the crowded field of battle'.

Where did Graham Young acquire his knowledge of poisons and like substances? He read a lot. Brendan Hayden: 'I interviewed staff at Neasden library, North London. They remembered him coming in and getting books out on anything to do with toxicology. He was always interested in poisons and poisoners, like William Palmer. They even remembered him going out and getting the bread rolls from a local café.' It is as well he did not buy their cups of tea there as well.

Maxwell Day was a probationer police constable with just seven months' service when they called him into the station to take a prisoner to Brixton. 'What's he in for?' he asked the sergeant. 'Murder, son,' he was told. Mr Day, now retired, found Young offering boiled sweets to his colleagues. They were declined. In the prison van Young spoke of his admiration of Hitler and Hitler Youth. 'He went on and on about it,' says Mr Day. Even in custody on the most serious charge of all, Young couldn't help himself.

Graham Frederick Young stood trial at St Albans in June, 1972. The charges: two murders, two attempted murders and four counts of administering antimony. He pleaded Not Guilty on all counts. On the question of motive, counsel said, 'This man doesn't need a motive to poison people beyond the sheer fascination of watching the development of symptoms.' Of his admissions of guilt to police Young said he had 'given a plausible set of answers so that he could get clothing, food and sleep'. He confessed, he said, to enable the police to substantiate their charges and so leave him alone from further interrogation. He had given a 'compound' to Mr Biggs to be used in his garden to get rid of insects. He admitted buying thallium and antimony, and providing a false name, saying it was for private research. There were restrictions on the sale of poisons, by having to sign a form and have it countersigned, 'A time consuming and tiresome procedure so I took a short cut by using a false name.'

After one and a half hours the jury returned verdicts of 'Guilty' on all charges, except two of administering antimony. It was only then that the grim details of Young's previous convictions and incarceration at Broadmoor were made known to the jury. He was sentenced to life imprisonment. He died of heart disease, aged 42, in Parkhurst prison, by which time he was described by doctors as 'psychotically ill'.

RIGHT **On remand**
Constable Max Day escorts Young to a waiting prison van. Young's offer of boiled sweets was declined by police officers
Evening Echo

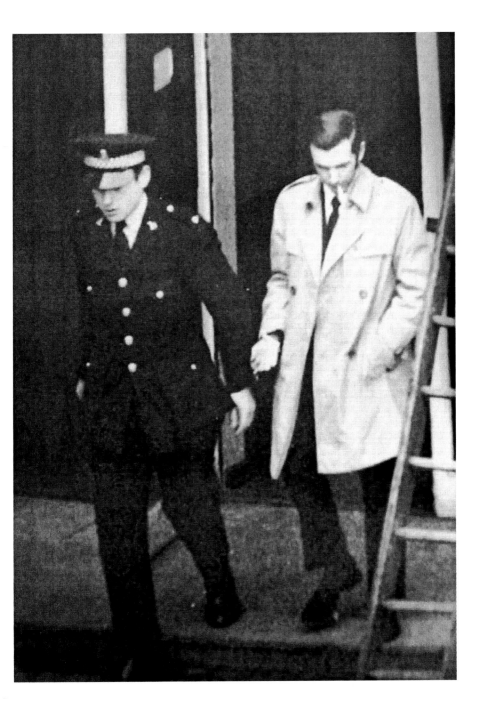

The Verdict

Graham Young was just three weeks old when he went to live with his aunt. At three years old he went to live with his father, who had remarried, and his stepmother. An unfortunate start to life, but he still had family to care for him. His father told police that Graham did not mix with other boys, but spent a lot of time reading. Young became intensely interested in chemistry; he brought home books on poison, which he disguised beneath the covers taken from other books. He was once found by police searching dustbins behind a chemist's shop.

A child reading books on poison may seem sinister, but there was nothing sinister when he read them as an adult. After all, the books had been written, they were intended to be read. Young's morbid interest in Nazi paraphernalia and Hitler and the macabre gave clues to his state of mind, but let it be said that others will take like-interest without murdering people.

Graham Young was what he was, a cruel and ruthless psychopath who, as a boy, poisoned members of his own family, including his mother, and a friend, and as an adult poisoned his workmates, in the latter case so skilfully he chose whom he intended to die or otherwise. He acted without any apparent or understandable motive other than to witness their suffering, and with utter disregard for human life. Life imprisonment, really for life, was the right sentence for such a man.

Freed to Kill

Graham Young was convicted of the most heinous crimes. But was he alone responsible? As his barrister said at the trial, 'It was only possible for Young to commit these offences because he was released from Broadmoor. This release may in the light of events be considered a serious error of judgement. The authorities had a duty to protect Graham Young from himself as well as from the public.'

At Young's earlier trial, in 1962, a senior medical officer told the Court he was a psychopath who needed care in a maximum security hospital. He was asked, 'Does this mean this behaviour will be repeated if he gets the opportunity?' He replied, 'It is extremely likely... I would say he is prepared to kill.' The Judge's recommendation was that Young be made subject of a Restriction Order for 15 years. Instead, he was released after just nine, first to visit his family, notwithstanding his family's own concerns, then to attend a Government Training Centre, after which he went to live and work in Hemel Hempstead.

There are two issues: why was Graham Young released in the first place; and why did the after-care service fail? In 1962, medical experts found it was impossible to establish 'real contact' with him, and that he was hostile to nursing staff and other patients and had to be put on tranquillisers. Yet, by 1964, it was considered he would benefit if he became a 'green card' inmate, and he was given the run of Broadmoor's grounds. In the opinion of the medical superintendent and the consultant psychiatrist, this increased freedom had beneficial effects. So in 1965 he was given his own room, which he promptly decorated with pictures of Adolph Hitler and other prominent Nazis.

By early 1966, Young was regarded as a model prisoner: alert, highly intelligent, eager to assist with his rehabilitation. By 1969 there had been a 'remarkable improvement'. In January, 1971, the Department of Health recommended his release on licence, and on 8th February he was free. He went to the Training Centre at Slough, itself a government institution, yet one which was not told why he had been in Broadmoor. His subsequent employers, Hadlands, were not told he had been in Broadmoor at all. Also, it was the rule that when a patient was released from Broadmoor, the police in the area where he would reside should be told. They were not. The system was in place but it was not adhered to.

The Probation Officer to whom Young had to report after his release went neither to his workplace nor to his home. If he had gone to the latter he would have found ample evidence, as the police did, of Young's continuing obsession with Nazi-ism and the macabre. Once free, Young was at liberty to poison anyone. He drank in the King Harry public house in Hemel Hempstead, where he could have randomly slipped poison into anyone's drink. Since he evidently enjoyed the sight of seeing his victims suffer over time, this was probably unlikely. Instead, he poisoned his workmates. He would have found their pain and suffering satisfying to witness.

The then Home Secretary, Reginald Maudling, said, 'What haunts me is the dilemma of Broadmoor. What do you do with people whom doctors say are safe to let out, but who have a violent record? Do you keep them in, and destroy them? Or do you take an expert's word and accept a possible risk to society?' A terrible responsibility, to be sure. But it could be removed by applying a simple rule that anyone who poisons another person should never be free to do so again. Graham Young was set free to embark upon a mission of death. Those who freed him, despite evidence that suggested he would kill, must take responsibility too.

12

An Appallingly Dangerous Man

Nomansland 1977

The Murder of Janie Shepherd

On Monday, 18th April, 1977, two young boys from St Albans were out on their bikes on Nomansland Common, near Wheathampstead. It was the Easter school holidays, and about 5.30 p.m. that day as they wheeled their bikes through thick bracken they came across what looked like a bundle of rags, partly covered by sticks and leaves about twenty yards from the B651, a place known as Devil's Dyke, about quarter of a mile from the Wicked Lady public house. When they looked closer they saw skin and ran off, but returned at once and when they looked again they saw blonde hair. They hurried home and told their parents who told the police.

The remains were quickly identified as 24-year-old Janie Shepherd, a young Australian woman who had been missing since for ten weeks from her home in St John's Wood, London. Her parents, her friends and relatives and the police had all suspected that something terrible had happened to Janie, and their fears were proved correct on the discovery of her decomposing body on the Common. Janie had been murdered, and her body had been dumped where it was found. It would take three police investigations and twelve years before her alleged killer was arrested and convicted for an appalling crime perpetrated upon a young woman who had everything to live for.

Janie Shepherd was gregarious, beautiful and happy. Her stepfather and mother, Mr and Mrs Darling, lived in Australia, but Janie loved London and she had decided to live and work there. She had lived on and off with her cousin and her husband at their luxury home in St John's Wood since 1971. She worked at an art gallery in Westbourne Grove, and enjoyed swimming and dancing. She had a boyfriend, Roddy Kinkead-Weekes, a county cricketer. One can imagine her daily routine: home, work, boyfriend and a full social life. It would all end abruptly and horrifically on Friday, 4th February, 1977.

That evening Janie left her cousin's house at 8.40, saying she 'must dash'. She was bound for her boyfriend's flat in Knightsbridge. She was wearing jeans tucked into Cossack-style boots, a man's shirt over a thin polo-necked sweater and a white cardigan. She carried a big satchel-style bag containing a change of clothing – a black sweater with green cuffs, and clean underwear. She also wore items of expensive jewellery, including a 'Woodstock' charm attached to a necklace.

She would drive there in her Mini, registration number KGM 300P, but not before calling at the Europa Foodstore in Queensway, west London. She bought some groceries, but did not arrive at her boyfriend's flat. As the evening wore on he became worried, calling hospitals, then the police, finally reporting her missing at 3.45 a.m. The police routinely noted her description and circulated details, including those of her Mini, which had a 'For Sale' sign in the rear window. The car was found four days later in Elgin Crescent, Notting Hill, near Ladbroke Grove. Enquiries revealed it had been there since the early hours of 5th February, just hours after Janie's disappearance.

The appearance of the car almost certainly proved that something terrible had happed to Janie. It was covered in mud, with shreds of leaves and more mud in the wheel arches. The soft sunroof had been slashed twice with a sharp instrument, probably a knife. One seat belt had been cut through. There was clothing strewn all over the inside of the vehicle, along with Janie's Cossack boots and the satchel-style

Miss Janie Shepherd

bag. Her change of clothing was missing. A single black, Negroid hair was found in the vehicle. Some of the foodstuffs she had bought were partly eaten and were scattered in gardens near to where the car was found. Calculating the mileage from a recent petrol receipt, police deducted that the car had been driven about 75 miles. When forensic scientists examined the mud and leaves they concluded that the car had been driven on chalky soil, where beech, oak and hawthorn grew. Somewhere like the Chiltern Hills, for example. The police sent up helicopters in a vain search for a newly-dug grave.

Janie's parents flew to England. Having been informed that her car had possibly been 'on chalky soil', they bought Ordnance Survey maps and searched for Janie themselves. For over two months they drove the Chiltern byways. How determined their search, but how futile. They, like everyone, thought the worst must have happened, that Janie had been raped, murdered, taken away and buried somewhere. Finally, after ten weeks they went home to Australia. One can imagine their feelings as they reluctantly had to accept that they would never see their daughter again.

Detective Chief Superintendent Henry Mooney of the Metropolitan Police took charge. He was an experienced and skilled detective. Later, he would famously say that 'investigating a murder without a body is like looking down the wrong end of a telescope'. That is what the Metropolitan Police were conducting, a murder enquiry, even though Janie had not then been found. One thing the police had discovered: a woman who lived near the spot where Janie parked that night had heard 'a desperate, strangled cry of a woman...'. She later went out and found a potato-peeling knife, which she handed to police after she read of the discovery of the body in April.

DCS Mooney focused on suspects. That's what the police do when an offender's identity isn't obvious; they look at those with 'form' who have committed similar crimes. One came straight into the frame. He was David Ronald Lashley, otherwise known as The Beast of Shepherd's Bush. He was 37 years old, a car sprayer from Southall and native of Barbados, a man with an appalling record of committing sexual offences against women. Even so, investigating detectives might have been forgiven if they thought, despite Lashley's 'form', he was not their man. In 1970, he had been convicted at the Old Bailey of three rapes, two indecent assaults and a robbery, for which he had been sentenced to a total of 12 years' imprisonment. It was this series of attacks on women that earned Lashley the 'Beast' nickname. He would drive around west London preying on women motorists. Although big in stature, Lashley favoured small cars, presumably because his victims could be overpowered in a confined space. After his conviction, his blonde wife divorced him, which may have motivated him afterwards to 'hate white, blonde women'. The judge told him on that occasion, 'You behaved like an animal without thought of the damage physically

158

David Lashley

and psychologically that you might do... There does not appear to be any reason to suppose you would not behave in that way again.' So, having been sent down for twelve years, and taking into account the judge's remarks, he couldn't be free after serving just half of his sentence — could he?

He could, and he was. Released in March, 1976, barely three months later he attacked another woman, a blonde known as Miss A. She had parked near Ladbroke Grove, London, in her Renault, when Lashley pounced. He tied her wrists, then drove her to the Notting Hill area where he tore off her clothes, raped her twice and told her he would have to kill her. Then he grabbed her throat and started to choke her, pushing hard on her windpipe. Finally, he cut her wrist, severing an artery, and said, 'Die, you white bitch, die.' He left her then, to die, presumably. But Miss A was somehow able to drive, using one hand to steer and holding the other up to try and stem the blood-flow. She drove to the area where she lived, and neighbours called for an ambulance and the police. On the very day Janie Shepherd's body was found on Nomansland Common, Lashley was being committed for trial by magistrates in London for this attack. In December, 1977, he was convicted for attempted murder, rape and other offences on Miss A and sentenced to 18 years. The judge told him, 'You are without doubt the most evil sex attacker ever to set foot in the Old Bailey. Your attack on this woman was a carbon copy of your previous crimes.' It was between his release in March, 1976, and being arrested on 17th February, 1977 for the attack on Miss A, that Lashley was free and very much in the frame for the murder of Janie Shepherd.

In fact, he was questioned about Janie just eight days after her disappearance, and a week later he was charged with the attempted murder and double rape of Miss A. But when it came to questioning him about Janie Shepherd, the police had nothing to go on other than suspicion. They could not even at that time say that Janie was dead, as her body had not been found. With no evidence against Lashley, the case had to be dropped. Things changed when Janie's body was discovered. Now police could establish cause of death, and piece together evidence concerning her death, and other information, gathered about the time of her disappearance:

Firstly, Janie was fully clothed, but she was not wearing the same clothes she wore when she had left her cousin's house on the night of 4th February. Instead she had been dressed, probably after death, in the black sweater with green cuffs, part of the spare clothing she had intended to take to her boyfriend's for the weekend. Her jewellery, including the 'Woodstock' charm and necklace, had not been removed, and helped in the initial process of identification.

Second, her upper arms had been strapped across her chest, and her feet had been tied together before death. She had extensive bruising to the upper arms, and one buttock had been mutilated with a knife, which had been thrust through her jeans. Her face and body were bruised, suggesting she had struggled with her attacker. A number of 'pinprick' wounds on both breasts appeared as though they had been made by fingernails. She had almost certainly been raped, although decomposition of the body could not conclusively establish this. Formal identification was by dental records. Cause of death was severe compression of the windpipe, consistent with a fist being forcibly rammed into her throat.

In addition to the above, police had tracked down a married couple who had driven behind Janie's Mini along King's Langley High Street on the night she disappeared. They remembered it because the number was similar to the initials of the husband. They noticed that the blonde woman passenger appeared drunk, as she seemed to fall sideways as the car was driven along the road. The implication was that Janie was dead at that time, and that her assailant had strapped her in an upright position as he drove to the spot where he would dump her body, having re-dressed her after tearing her clothing from her during the attack.

Responsibility for conducting what was now a confirmed murder enquiry now transferred to Hertfordshire Constabulary. A fresh team of detectives had to sift through statements and other information hitherto gathered by the Metropolitan Police. Now on remand in prison for his attack on Miss A, Lashley refused to be interviewed. Detectives would have sought to build a case based on forensic evidence, but there was none: no semen or spillage of blood for grouping, no fingerprints in the car, no 'contamination', such as fibres of the murderer's clothing. There was just that one Negroid hair, not sufficient in those days to classify for DNA. One further piece of circumstantial evidence pointing to Lashley was that he may have been familiar with Nomansland Common, having been to the area often enough to visit his wife's son at a children's home at Harpenden. But there wasn't enough evidence to charge him, and the case was wound down, although not 'closed', as they say. Lashley, meanwhile, being convicted of the attack on Miss A, began his 18-year sentence for that crime alone. The murder of Janie Shepherd remained unsolved – until twelve years later, when the police re-examined the file and notified the authorities at Frankland prison, near Durham, where Lashley was incarcerated, of their continuing interest in him. As a result, when prison staff received certain information from a serving prisoner, the police were contacted.

The prisoner was Daniel Reece, a 32-year-old Londoner, who was serving 13 years for rape. Reece, in fact, had earlier been a 'supergrass', someone who admits his crimes and blows the whistle on other criminals – giving Queen's Evidence – in return (usually) for certain privileges whilst in prison, a shorter sentence and, ultimately, to ensure his own safety thereafter, a new identity. Thus, Reece was not his real name. Having secured early release, he re-offended, this time raping the wife of a former business associate, at gunpoint, then committing a sexual offence on the man's son. In due course Reece and Lashley met in Frankland Prison.

Lashley was prompted to mention Janie Shepherd to Reece when he (Lashley) read about a black man who had been given a long prison sentence for rape. He said if he had killed her, the man would not have been caught.

Reece had never heard of Janie Shepherd. But Lashley didn't only mention her, he told Reece in vivid detail all about the crime: that he had seen a 'nice looking blonde girl' get out of a Mini and go into a shop in Queensway, west London; that he had noticed her car had a 'For Sale' notice in the window which he used as an excuse to speak to her; that he forced her into the car at knifepoint; that he had driven to Ladbroke Grove, parked up and torn her clothes off, tied her wrists together, slashed the roof of the car with the knife, and raped and strangled her. He even demonstrated how he had strangled her, holding the back of Reece's head with one hand, and forcing his fist against his windpipe with the other. He went on to say he re-dressed the body with Janie's spare clothes, strapped her to the front passenger seat and drove to Hertfordshire and threw her into some bushes. He had laughed as Janie's body swayed from side to side as he drove. The Mini got stuck in the mud, he said, but he freed it and drove back to the Ladbroke Grove area, eating the food Janie had bought. Then he dumped the car and went home to bed.

Lashley's account was told to Reece in May, 1988, eleven years after Janie's murder. Reece could not possibly have known any of these accurate details, in particular the precise manner in which Janie had died. He told a prison officer what Lashley had told him. This may seem strange, for he was a convicted rapist himself. It seems he regarded his own crime as a 'justifiable' act of revenge against someone who had had an affair with his wife, but that Lashley's abduction, rape and murder of the 'nice looking blonde girl' was too much to take. Even so, he was reluctant to talk to the police, but he did so, recounting the story to a Metropolitan Police detective whom he knew and trusted.

Eleven years on, the situation regarding policemen and witnesses had changed. The man now in post in Hertfordshire was Detective Superintendent Ian Whinnett, who, together with Detective Constable Mick Farendon, would now take charge of the investigation, the third into Janie's abduction, rape and murder. Det Con Farendon had the unenviable task of tracing Lashley's victims of 1969, twenty years before, those women who had been attacked in 'small cars', to prove 'similar fact' at the forthcoming trial. Fortunately there was time, for Lashley was safely ensconced in prison. He was due for release in February, 1989 – having served twelve years of the eighteen to which he had been sentenced – and he would have been looking forward to his forthcoming freedom. His freedom, when it came, was short-lived, for when he emerged from the gates of Frankland prison carrying his suitcases he was promptly arrested. Three days later he was charged. He never admitted the crime, and there was no forensic evidence to speak of, but he would now stand trial.

Reece was not the only prisoner to whom Lashley had 'confessed'. In 1981, in less detail, he had also told another man, when the pair

Ex-Detective Superintendent Ian Whinnett

met in Wakefield Prison. A convicted murderer came forward when he heard of Lashley's arrest. Lashley had told him he had only himself to blame for being caught, saying he should have 'dumped the body like I did'. The man told police, 'He (Lashley) said he got into the girl's car with a knife and threatened her. They had sex and a scuffle took place. He hit the girl and held her captive with the strap of her handbag. He strangled her and dumped the body.' Another man, who was in prison with Lashley in 1977–78, asked Lashley if it was correct that he had killed a girl? Lashley said it was, and they would never prove it. When he heard that Lashley had been arrested, he came forward with this information.

As well as the testimony of three convicted criminals, there was circumstantial evidence against David Lashley. First, Janie had cleaned her Mini on the evening of her disappearance, as she intended to sell it. She was not known to eat peanuts or chew gum, yet such items were found in her car, as they were in Lashley's own vehicle, a van. Lashley admitted eating peanuts and chewing gum (about the only thing he did admit, but then he did allege DCS Mooney had 'planted' the nuts and gum in Janie's car). Second, the potato peeling knife which had been found by the woman resident near to where Janie's car was discovered, was exactly the same as one which had gone missing from the canteen of a removals company, just before Janie's murder, where Lashley had been working at the time. Third, that piece of Negroid hair, found in Janie's car. Alas, although DNA had recently been introduced, the samples of twelve years ago were too 'degraded' to be of use. DNA would play no part in the case against David Lashley.

On 27th February, 1990, David Lashley stood trial at St Albans Crown Court. He pleaded Not Guilty. The Judge was Justice Alliott. For the prosecution, Mr Michael Kalisher told the Court that Janie Shepherd was 'an attractive, vivacious, healthy young woman of independent means'. He said that Lashley had demonstrated to Daniel Reece how he killed her as he raped her, an overwhelming piece of evidence because she was killed in an unusual way and the demonstration entirely agreed with the pathologist's report on her death. He went on, 'The Crown will contend that the confession (to Reece) was so detailed, so accurate and so consistent with the known facts it could only have come from the murderer himself. It is

---

The Verdict

It is difficult to imagine a more horrific crime than this, perpetrated upon a young woman happily going about her daily life. There she was, finished work and off to see her boyfriend for the weekend, full of life, full of anticipation, when she encounters a monster, a man bent on having his own way with her, who abducts, beats and rapes her, and murders her by crushing her throat with his fist. A particular odious aspect of this crime is the thought of her lifeless body, strapped upright in her Mini, swaying as she was driven out of London before being dumped among the bushes of Nomansland Common. How her relatives must have hated the sight of the powerfully built man as he stood in the dock, as the gruesome circumstances of Janie Shepherd's death were revealed. But Lashley's undoubted fearful presence was not evidence against him, nor indeed was any of the emotion his presence will have generated in the courtroom.

It was the rule then that an accused person's criminal history, if any, was to be kept from the jury until after their verdict. This was to ensure they were not swayed by circumstances that have nothing to do with the present case. So the jury would not have known that David Lashley had previously been sentenced to twelve years and then eighteen years for a series of rapes and sexual assaults, and attempted murder and two more rapes. Yet in this case they would have known

overwhelming and too horrifying to be anything other than the truth. He (Reece) had no other source of such information...'

It was for the defence to now discredit Reece. Apart from attacking his character — and there was plenty to attack, he being a convicted

---

Lashley did have a criminal record, for the evidence of Daniel Reece and others was that they had heard Lashley speaking of what he did *in prison*. Was the judgement of the jury thus contaminated? Without doubt the judge, not to mention Lashley's own barrister, would have said suitable words on this point. Something like, 'Put the fact that Mr Lashley has been in prison from your minds and focus solely on the evidence you have heard.' Quite right; after all, he could have been in prison for stealing cars or fraud.

There was scant evidence, aside from the testimonies of serving criminals. No admissions, virtually no forensic evidence and no fingerprints. There was the potato-peeling knife, almost certainly the one taken from the place where Lashley worked and found near the scene of the crime. The Negroid hair. The prosecution were obliged to rely heavily on the testimonies of men whose integrity would have been attacked head-on by the defence. They were doing it for favours, such as better conditions in prison. They were doing it for personal reasons, such as having been bullied by Lashley. They were doing it for money. Reece, himself serving time for rape and a man of previous 'supergrass' status, would have been especially their target. Yet he was able to give an accurate account of the details of Janie's murder. What he and the others said Lashley had told them was true, all of it. They told the jury things they could only have learned from the killer. The jury was satisfied and returned a Guilty verdict. Who could blame them?

---

rapist — they would have suggested he testified to acquire favours and/or payment. Reece stood his ground and denied any of these things. He had told the truth, he said. And wasn't his description of events, courtesy of Lashley, accurate? The only other defence offered by Lashley was that of his uncle and aunt, with whom he lived. They both testified, saying he was at home on the night in question. He could have spoken in his own defence, but chose to say nothing. The testimony of Reece, and the circumstantial evidence to go with it, was enough for the jury, who either disbelieved Lashley's uncle and aunt, or considered them mistaken. They took just over two hours to return a Guilty verdict. Sentencing Lashley to life imprisonment, the judge told him, 'You are such an appallingly dangerous man that the real issue is whether the authorities can ever allow you your liberty.' Quite so, but hadn't we heard similar words before?

In 1994 Lashley appealed against his conviction. The content of the appeal is technical, and in keeping with what one expects after any conviction. Refusing the appeal, the judges referred, among other things, to the fact that Lashley had chosen not to give evidence to 'undermine, controvert or explain the evidence from the Crown'. Nearly 17½ years after the most dreadful crimes perpetrated upon a young woman, David Ronald Lashley went back to his prison cell. Could he ever be freed, on a further appeal perhaps? Could he ever be released, on parole? If, as the jury decided, he was indeed guilty, society must pray that he is not.

Early Release from Detention

This case bears similarities to that of the Bovingdon poisoner, Graham Young, six years before. Both offenders were sentenced to long periods of detention; both were released to commit serious crimes of murder or attempted murder and, in Lashley's case, rape. Graham Young was released from a mental hospital, David Lashley from prison.

What is prison for? Three principal reasons: to protect society from offenders, to punish and to rehabilitate. The first two seem straightforward: when someone is locked up they cannot be committing crime on the outside, and let the punishment fit the crime, as they say. Rehabilitation is another matter. In almost all cases, a serving prisoner will be released someday, with or without remission. Sadly, many go on to re-offend. Still, they are given the chance, and that must be right, in the interests of society as well as themselves. Those convicted of non-violent crimes ordinarily pose no threat of violence. But there are 'degrees' of violence, and those at the top of the scale – some murderers, rapists, paedophiles – should fall into a category of their own which ensures they will never be released.

David Lashley was a repeat offender. In 1969, he had prowled around London looking for women whom he attacked and raped or sexually assaulted. He was sentenced to twelve years, and released after serving only half of his sentence. He was thus able to carry out another horrific attack, when he attempted to murder and twice raped a woman, for which he was sentenced to eighteen years but released after twelve.

On each occasion, his victims and their families had the satisfaction of seeing David Lashley being sentenced to long terms of imprisonment. Then they were let down utterly by a system that allowed his early release. He got twelve years, he should have served twelve years. He got eighteen years, he should have served eighteen years. And after all that, having been convicted of rape and murder, he got life and he should serve life. What system is it that allows the release of such men anyway? Who, precisely, makes the decision? Politicians, psychiatrists, medical people, whoever, they should all be accountable. One wonders whether they should stand in the dock alongside the man they see fit to release, so that victims and their families can witness all aspects of the case brought to conclusion. That should focus minds.

13

"WITH CONSIDERABLE COURAGE"

Hemel Hempstead 1988

The Murder of PC Frank Mason

There are certain events which, when they happen, are so tragic, so poignant, that henceforth they are etched forever in our minds, never to be erased no matter what. Such an event took place on Thursday, 14th April, 1988, and if the exact date is not recalled by police and civilian staff of the Hertfordshire Constabulary who were in post at that time, the event itself will be, for this was the day Frank Mason, a 27-year-old copper with four years' service, was murdered on the pavement outside Barclays Bank, at Bank Court, Hemel Hempstead.

Francis John Mason was married and lived in St John's Road, Boxmoor. He was off duty at the time, walking his dog, when by chance he came upon an armed robbery outside the bank. It was about 10 a.m. Approaching from the direction of Waterhouse Street, he would have seen a security van and a man pointing a gun at a guard. Without hesitation, PC Mason jumped on the gunman's back in an attempt to thwart the robbery and disarm him. He may have succeeded, except that a second gunman stepped forward and shot him in the back at close range. As Mr Michael Kalisher, QC, would tell the jury at Southwark Crown Court, 'He saw the robbery taking place and with considerable courage, because he must have seen they were armed, decided to tackle the parties.' Considerable courage indeed, but

Frank Mason paid for it with his life.

He had been shot with a Colt revolver. The robbers and their getaway driver escaped with £15,480 in cash and cheques worth £86,000. They hijacked a car and drove to Adeyfield, where a changeover vehicle was waiting for them to make good their escape from the town.

Sara Jones, 29, a nurse, was also off duty that morning. She was in the vicinity with her boyfriend. They had just driven into Bank Court when they noticed lots of people on the pavements and leaning from windows. Then they saw PC Mason's Collie dog running off, dragging its lead. Ms Jones asked someone what was happening and was told a man had been shot. She got out of the car and went to the scene where she saw PC Mason on the pavement. A first aid box, brought from one of the banks, lay beside him. She could see he was seriously injured; he had lost a lot of blood from the wound in his back, which a man was trying to stop with a pressure bandage. She put her jacket on PC Mason, who was semi-conscious, and gave him cardiac massage while a male nurse gave mouth to mouth resuscitation. His pulse became stronger but she knew he was 'slipping away'.

When the ambulance came she helped place PC Mason on to the trolley. Later, Ms Jones, who had ten years' experience as a nurse, would tell the *Hemel Hempstead Gazette* that although she had seen and coped with death and terrible injuries she was unprepared for the horror of that day. 'I've never attended anyone in the street. I've never seen a road accident. I worked almost mechanically when I was there (at the scene) but it didn't sink in until later how awful it was.' PC Mason was taken to West Herts Hospital, Hemel Hempstead, where he died of his injuries.

The robbers' getaway was almost thwarted by another act of courage. Mr Mansel Davies, 54, a caretaker at the John F. Kennedy School, had just come out of the bank when he heard the shot. When he saw the robbers being driven off he got into his own car and gave chase through the town's traffic, and tried to ram their vehicle. He kept sounding his horn. A man in the back of the car kept looking back

Police Constable Frank Mason

and when the car stopped the robbers jumped out. Mr Davies thought they were coming after him, but then he saw them wave a gun at the driver of a passing car, which they hijacked.

A council employee, Mr Ray Swan, was working nearby when he heard the shot and saw the robbers run to their getaway car shouting 'Go-Go-Go.' He saw they were carying guns, and watched as the getaway car narrowly avoided an approaching van by mounting the pavement. Mr Swan then helped to try and revive PC Mason. A spokesman for Securicor stated that there was no money outside the van, but in the life-threatening situation that had developed three bagfuls were deposited into the bank chute for the robbers to take. It was then that PC Mason intervened. The money and cheques were seized by the robbers before they fled.

The robbers had escaped with their loot. But they wouldn't be free for long. Regional Crime Squad officers knew who they were, knew where they were from and knew where they were going. Which is not to say they could have prevented the crime. They had known all along of the robbers' intentions, and had built up 'intelligence' over a period of time to hopefully arrest them before their intended crime was committed. If the tragic events on the day meant the loss of life of one of their colleagues, they would at least deal swiftly with his killers.

Surveillance of known or suspected criminals is a tool of the Regional Crime Squad – the RCS. It is what they do, either by observing criminals' behaviour, or by following them, by car or on foot, or both. They also rely on 'information', gained by whatever means, to help with their intelligence gathering process. So it was with the killers of PC Mason. Officers of the 'Regional' had been observing them for some time, at Luton.

The gang comprised several members. They included Charles McGhee, 30 years; Perry Wharrie, 28; James Hurley, 26; and Robert McFarland, 32. The RCS had the information and the intelligence, and had earlier approached the Crown Prosecution Service with a view to arresting the gang for conspiracy to rob, a desirable course of action which, if successful, removes criminals from the streets before they commit serious crimes. Information and intelligence alone are not evidence, however, and after considering the information put before them the CPS decided there was insufficient evidence to make arrests that would probably end in failure. To get the evidence the RCS would have to find it. This is what they were about in the period up to and including that fateful day at Hemel Hempstead. Their operation was over two planned phases: an intelligence gathering process, and mobile surveillance.

Gathering 'intelligence' is a painstaking process, which takes time and patience. Basically, the 'targets' were observed. They were known to possess at least two stolen cars, and a third on false number plates. Arresting them in stolen vehicles was hardly appropriate, considering the robberies they were suspected of committing. Mobile surveillance depends entirely on the actions of the 'targets', and will obviously not take place if they don't go anywhere. So it was before the day of PC Mason's murder: the 'targets' were static. Just the same, the Squad had attached a tracker device on to one of the 'target' vehicles. This would send a signal to an unmarked police vehicle, which would then be able to follow at a discreet distance, and hopefully other officers could swoop on the 'targets' to catch them in the act of committing crime. Such a procedure is not undertaken lightly, and special permission was sought before a tracking device was used.

The 'target' car was bugged for a fortnight, during which time it didn't move. But inactivity doesn't last forever, and at 9.35 a.m. on 14th April, the day of the shooting, the suspects' car, with the tracking device fitted, suddenly went mobile. It was driven by James Hurley, the getaway driver. Also in the car were McGhee and Wharrie. They drove at speed, from an address in Luton down the A1081, the former A6, through Harpenden, arriving at Hemel Hempstead at 9.50 a.m. Regional Crime Squad officers, relying on the tracking vehicle, followed, but could not responsibly keep up with the pace.

Barclays Bank, Bank Court, Hemel Hempstead

To have done so, particularly through highly populated towns such as Harpenden and Hemel Hempstead, was not a lawful option. There was, too, the risk that if police got too close they would be spotted and their operation thwarted. Consequently the gang arrived at Bank Court in advance of the pursing police.

Even so, the Squad, some of whom were armed, did not consider this to be a problem. They knew a Securicor vehicle was not due at Bank Court until ten to fifteen minutes later, and they would be in position by that time. When they arrived in Hemel Hempstead they parked up, ready to deal with events, not knowing that, by chance, another Securicor vehicle was already in situ in Bank Court. Clearly, one was as good as another for the robbers, only for PC Mason, off duty and unaware of events, to appear with tragic consequences. After their subsequent escape, McGhee, Wharrie and Hurley, still unaware of the Regional Crime Squad's presence, sped back to base at Richmond Hill, Luton.

Later, at Crown Court, prosecuting counsel told the jury how PC Mason had grappled with a gunman on the pavement. 'That was Mr Wharrie,' he said, adding that 'McGhee, seeing the struggle, decided to shoot PC Mason.' He explained that after the murder, Regional Crime Squad officers had staked out the shop at Luton, where, two hours later McFarland arrived carrying a holdall, and after going inside emerged carrying some dustbin liners. Then he and Hurley went to a lock-up garage in Wardown Crescent, also Luton, which was also under police surveillance. When they went inside the lock-up they were arrested, and police found guns and ammunition inside. This included the two revolvers used at Bank Court, as well as a sub-machine gun and ammunition. Soon after that McGhee and Wharrie emerged from the flat to take a taxi they had sent for, and were arrested carrying most of the stolen money.

McGhee, Wharrie and Hurley, the getaway driver, were convicted of murdering PC Mason, as well as robbery and firearms offences. It is always the case that where criminals act jointly that all are equally guilty of the crime. The court was told that McGhee was 'a pathological hater of police'. They all received life sentences, in McGhee's case with the recommendation that he serve a minimum of eighteen years. It was a condition he would not fulfil, for he died in prison. Hurley escaped custody after serving five years. McFarland was sentenced to three years for conspiracy.

Until this incident, police use of 'bugging devices' on suspects' cars was largely unknown, to public and criminals alike. This case was the first time such tactics were disclosed in open court. From now on, active criminals would be aware, through the case being reported in

---

The Verdict

Off duty, in plain clothes, out for a walk with his dog. Did Frank Mason do the right thing when he chanced upon an armed robbery? Did he see a gunman and 'have a go', unaware there was a second armed man nearby, a man described as 'a pathological hater of police'? Barclays Bank could have stood the loss. No-one until that moment had been hurt although, let it be said, someone might yet have been. Many of Frank's peers will say he should have stepped back and observed, to be a valuable witness later – and yet, put in the same situation, they would have done exactly as he did. Frank was a copper: he saw what he saw, he did what he did. His were the actions of a brave man. Which is more than can be said for the man who stepped forward and shot him in the back at close range. This crime highlights the danger police men and women face, anywhere, anytime. Frank's memorial merits more than 'Here fell...', surely.

---

the newspapers, and even drama on television, that a check in their rear-view mirrors may no longer betray a squad car on their tail. But in their efforts to catch so-called professional criminals, one wonders where the police stand when using such equipment in today's climate of 'human rights'. Criminals' rights, more like. Does anyone imagine they fix them to the cars of law-abiding citizens?

Frank Mason was only 27 when he was murdered. He and his wife, Gill, had no children. He lived and worked in Hemel Hempstead and was known to many local people, including traders, in the town. Tributes from those who knew him included 'unassuming', 'dedicated'

Charles McGhee was sentenced to life imprisonment, with a recommendation that he serve a minimum of eighteen years. Why so? There was a time he would have hanged for murder; now, after such a brutal crime, he would be able to look forward to his liberty again. This is the law, but this is not justice. Justice would be to lock such men up for good. They who would carry guns and murder in the furtherance of personal gain, let them do so in the knowledge that if they are caught they will never be released.

Perry Wharrie and James Hurley were also convicted of murder. Yet Charles McGee, not they, shot PC Mason. It has always been that where two or more people act 'in concert' they are all guilty; but were they all acting 'in concert' here? Unless either of the others called out for McGhee to pull the trigger, then neither would have had control over McGhee's actions. If McGhee, seeing his companion struggling with a member of the public, took it upon himself to pull the trigger, then had he alone, not Wharrie or Hurley, committed murder? Here lies the value of the jury system: let the facts be put, let twelve men and women good and true decide. The jury decided they were all guilty of murder. So be it.

---

and a 'very nice chap'. He was awarded the Queen's Gallantry medal for his bravery, and a memorial to him was unveiled in Bank Court, on the spot where he was killed. The inscription says, simply, 'Here fell PC Frank Mason'. Nothing of the circumstances, of his bravery that day when, unarmed and off duty, he attempted to thwart an armed robbery. Didn't he deserve more?

"Not afraid to do his duty"

PC Frank Hulme

Police officers have a dangerous job. Some are killed, sometimes in a deliberate act of murder, as was Frank Mason, and sometimes through being involved in incidents where an unlawful act culminates in the death of an officer. One such case occurred late one November night in 1958, when two or more groups of men became involved in a drunken brawl, and one of the two constables who stepped in to sort it out received fatal injuries. Again the town was Hemel Hempstead; again the officer who died was called Frank.

Frank Edwin Hulme was 31, a married man who lived with his wife and three children in Turners Hill, Hemel Hempstead. He was a Lancashire lad who had joined 'the job', in 1952. That night he was on duty in the High Street in the Old Town. It was closing time, and the pubs were turning out. A group of drunks had been ejected from the Royal Oak for fighting, and now they were on the street. Other pubs were turning out too, and it seems at least one other group of men were up for a fight. Whatever the exact circumstances, a 'long and violent struggle' ensued between at least two groups, and PC Hulme would have seen it as his job to do something about it.

He was joined by Constable James Homer who, dealing with a fight of his own, saw PC Hulme struggling with three men. He saw PC Hulme fall onto the steps of a shop, with two men on top of him. As usual in these situations, who actually did what to whom would have been unclear. Nor would things have been helped by 'witnesses' who were also drunk (and some of whom turned 'hostile' at the subsequent court hearing). PC Hulme was seen to be clutching his stomach. He was taken to West Herts Hospital, and two days later transferred to the Whittington Hospital, London, where he died on 12th December. At the funeral service at St Barnabas' Church, Adeyfield, the Rev Peter

Police Constable Frank Hulme

Stokes described PC Hulme as 'a man of simple tastes, direct and straightforward, a brave man who died because he was not afraid to do his duty.'

Four men appeared at Berkhamsted Magistrates' Court. At first, all four were charged with manslaughter. Then the court was told that PC Hulme, although in apparently good health, had unknowingly been suffering from an aneurysm of the brain, a sort of enlargement of an artery. He had always been liable to die suddenly because of this, although his death was actually caused by a blood clot leaving a bruised thigh, and moving through the bloodstream to a lung.

Two men were finally indicted on the manslaughter charge, whilst all four were charged with affray. They appeared at the Old Bailey in January, 1959. The prosecution offered no evidence on the manslaughter charges, and likewise offered none on charges of grievous bodily harm. Prosecution counsel explained that PC Hulme 'was always liable to sudden death,' implying, it seems, that this fact could not have been known to anyone who assaulted him. It is the opinion of the author that a man who assaults another should be responsible for his actions, notwithstanding the health of the victim. In any case, as the court was told, the blood clot, not the aneurysm of the brain, was the cause of death.

Three of the men pleaded guilty to affray. One, with three previous convictions for GBH, was told by the judge, that he was 'a violent young man' and sentenced to four months imprisonment. A second was given a 12-month conditional discharge, and a third was fined £10. The fourth was acquitted. Not Guilty pleas in respect of various assault charges against both constables were accepted by the court. Constables Hulme and Homer did their duty in difficult if not impossible circumstances that November night. Whether those in the criminal justice system did theirs is a matter of opinion.

Aged 18 years, PC Rayner was killed on 13th October 1982, when the male driver of a car which had 'failed to stop' for police, deliberately drove into the police vehicle in which she was seated. She was the youngest woman officer to be unlawfully killed in Britain. The driver of the car was sentenced to 5 years imprisonment for manslaughter.

Photo: 'Hertsbeat' Hertfordshire Constabulary.

Police Constable Mandy Rayner

Joan Macan

14

A Dastardly Crime

Ashridge Park 1988

The Murder of Joan Macan

It was her 81st birthday, but age had not wearied her. She was described as 'fearless', which she must have been, for Joan Macan had served her country with great bravery during the war when, under the code name 'Marie Baque', she worked with the resistance behind enemy lines in France, helping to smuggle out British airmen who had been shot down to escape over the Pyrenees into Spain. She won citations from Generals de Gaulle and Eisenhower, no less. But where she risked her life under the noses of the Gestapo nearly half a century before, where detection would have meant being shot as a spy, Joan Macan's cruel fate was to be murdered on the footpath in her own garden, an old lady struck down by cowards whom she had disturbed in the process of stealing her property.

This was a dastardly crime, committed by desperate men who, on being disturbed committing a burglary, had no hesitation in striking Mrs Macan on the head with a heavy object before making their escape. One can almost imagine the scene at her remote cottage in Ashridge Park, near Aldbury. Having parked her car in the garage, she was making her way along the flagged garden path when she encountered strangers. She would have had something to say to those who would enter her property, ne'er-do-wells of a different calibre to the airmen, French resistance personnel and herself who had fought in the cause of liberty.

Joan Macan's house stood on a hillside, surrounded by glorious beechwoods yet close enough to the edge of the park to afford grand views of the rolling Chilterns landscape beyond. She was into Labradors, with sixteen of her own, some of which were due to entered into a show at Birmingham that Saturday. That very year she had judged at Crufts, and the previous evening she had attended a dog show in Surrey. The attack occurred as she returned to her Ashridge home, where her lifeless body was discovered on the morning of Thursday, 5th May, 1988, by a neighbour. The blow to her head had killed her. Whatever weapon her attacker had used was not left at the scene. It may have been a spade, or similar implement.

When police attended the scene of the travesty they found the house had been ransacked. Burglary was the obvious motive. The thieves had entered the house by smashing a rear window. They would have rightly anticipated that there were valuable items inside, and would doubtless have made their escape by car, possibly by way of the access route from the end of Monument Drive. They would have been able to carry out their raid without being seen by neighbours, as the house is not overlooked. A public right of way passes alongside, but it is a quiet route and the house and gardens at the time were obscured from view by a high hedge.

Detecting this crime was never going to be straightforward. Mrs Macan lived alone, and there was uncertainty about what, precisely, had been stolen. There was no-one who might be able to provide details of a strange car. There was no forensic evidence, no fingerprints, no sign of any 'foreign' blood and no sign of the murder weapon or even any certainty, only speculation, as to what it might have been. The cause of death was the injury to Mrs Macan's head, an indisputable fact that pointed to murder.

It is usual at murder scenes for the police to carry out 'house to house' enquires to ascertain who, if anyone, saw anything, or knows anything, or can help in any way to trace and identify offenders. This was not possible at Ashridge Park, where houses are scattered and hidden from one another among the trees of National Trust woodland. So identifying the stolen property was of paramount importance, as a means of leading police to Mrs Macan's killers.

Mrs Macan had no children, but she did have a housekeeper who helped prepare a list of some of the stolen items. Four figurines in particular were identifiable: a bronze figure of a greyhound, eight inches high and dating from between 1824 to 1910, which was rare because it was usual for such an item to have two dogs on the base rather than one; a pointer dog with a hare in its mouth, with the artist's name, P.J. Mene, on the base and measuring eight inches high; a horse, also by Mene; and a setter pointing to a rabbit with a tree stump in the background, about seven inches tall and detached from the base.

Pierre Jules Mene was a French 19th-century sculptor, who is described as the most successful animal sculptor of his time. He was self-taught, and won First Class medals at the London Exhibitions of 1855 and 1861. He sculpted horses and dogs, especially racing and hunting types. So high was the quality of his bronze castings that other foundries tried to meet the same standards. It would follow, therefore, that the pointer dog with the hare in its mouth, and the horse, would be especially identifiable, if traced, as well as any other of Mene's objects if any had been stolen.

The list of known stolen property was extensive, 26 items at least. It included two clocks, a pair of marble bookends, a Japanese teapot, a number of small animal ornaments and silver snuff boxes of varying shapes and sizes. Of these, the clocks in particular were identifiable, one an antique wall-clock with gold-coloured scroll around the face; the other a 19th-century reproduction of an 18th-century French Cartel clock, with white face and Roman numerals. The stolen figures included a silver duck with hinged base, a metal-coloured emu, a silver rearing horse holding onto a shield, a bronze-coloured teddy bear lying on its stomach, and a silver llama with a pack on its back and two crossed ropes over the pack.

The police investigation took the form of an incident room, whose staff were led by Detective Chief Inspector Dick Pottinger. Enquires led to the identification of a number of suspects, members of the 'travelling' community who were believed to be committing crime in the area. These suspicions would turn out to be well-founded, when police made arrests for theft of and from motor vehicles, including at least one found burnt out at Ashridge about half a mile from the scene of the crime. Several admitted responsibility and were charged, although none could be connected with the murder of Joan Macan. Nevertheless, as experienced detectives will tell you, it is often the case that when investigating unrelated crime a vital breakthrough in a murder enquiry can follow; but detectives were disappointed when their endeavours in this regard led to nowhere except detecting unconnected offences.

Realising the importance of identifying and tracing the stolen property, the investigation team approached the BBC and the murder of Joan Macan appeared on 'Crimewatch'. Details of the stolen figurines were broadcast to the nation, as well as the grim details of the murder. One telephone call, one person somewhere who could identify one item of the stolen property, that's all the police needed for a possible breakthrough. Alas, no-one in the United Kingdom who watched the programme could help. As the police would admit, they had nowhere else to go, and the incident room was closed down. Which is not to say that the case was closed, as events proved six years later when two separate developments give fresh impetus to the case.

The first concerned information about a pond near Bovingdon known as Soldier's Bottom. There, it was said, three figurines had been dumped. To find them the pond would have to be drained, and when the police got the fire brigade to drain it they found an ornament, similar to that stolen from Mrs Macan's house. It turned out to be a brass figure of an animal. They thought it was one of the

Scene of crime revisited
Ex-Detective Chief Inspector Dick Pottinger led the police investigation

stolen figurines, but it wasn't. Even so, it could have been from the house; there were lots of ornaments stolen, maybe this was one of them. Police showed it to the housekeeper who could not identify it. They showed it to Mrs Macan's niece who lived in Berkshire, but she was not a frequent visitor to the house and she could neither say it was or was not the property of her aunt.

The second development concerned an unnamed social worker. She came forward with information about a conversation she had had during the course of her duties with a relative of someone the police had considered to be a possible witness at the murder scene, or even suspected of complicity, that is to say, present at the time of the crime and known to the killer, or killers. It concerned a woman we will identify as Molly.

Molly was one of the 'travelling' community, which is to say that the police would need to tread carefully when pursuing investigations. Insensitive pursuit of 'travellers' can lead to accusations of bias against people who are sometimes berated for their lifestyle. But this could not deter the police investigation, which was to investigate and detect the murder of Joan Macan. And so Molly was interviewed, with an educational welfare officer present to safeguard her rights. In days before tape recording interviews became routine, the interview was recorded. Police were acting to protect themselves and also in the interests of Molly.

Molly implicated her father and her boyfriend as being complicit in the murder. Her boyfriend, whom we shall know as John, she had been courting at the time. He and her father, she said, went into Mrs Macan's garden and committed the burglary, and it was they whom Mrs Macan had encountered on the garden path. Molly would not say which of them struck the blow that killed Mrs Macan. But she knew because she was present, standing by a gate in the picket fence which ran under the hedge, with another man we shall call Brian.

At first, DCI Pottinger and his colleagues didn't believe Molly's account. They too had visited the scene; they had examined it in detail and knew of no gate in the picket fence in the hedge. They knew only of the main entrance to the garden. They asked Molly to make a sketch of the scene, which she did and in which she clearly indicated a gate in the picket fence. Then detectives went back to the house, and when they pushed aside the branches of the thick hedge they found the gate, just as Molly had described. In fact, it turned out to be the former entrance to the garden. This was a crucial breakthrough; Molly, not the police, had identified the gate. She must have been there at some time to know about it. It would be at the time of the murder, surely.

Arrests followed, including the two main suspects and the man, Brian. Enquiries of other travellers then revealed that, on or about the day of the crime, Molly's father and John had been seen burning their clothing, which was probably bloodstained, to get rid of damning evidence against themselves. In consultation with the Crown Prosecution Service (CPS), the main suspects were charged and Molly would be used as a prosecution witness. The scene was set for an 'old style' committal, where evidence is given at the magistrates' court where, if the justices are satisfied that there is a case to answer, the accused will be remanded to the crown court for trial.

Although Molly had provided vital information to police, she was far from being a willing witness. Nevertheless she was brought to court to testify, but when she sat in the witness box the only thing she had to tell to the court was, 'I don't want to say anything.' A hostile witness, then, someone who was reluctant to testify but who could still be asked questions, who might still say something in connection with a murder enquiry, one which the police had worked so hard to crack and were still working on six years later. Alas, no. No sooner had Molly expressed her reluctance than the case was withdrawn. Molly left the court and took her testimony with her. A year later, one of the protagonists died, and the other was sent to prison for grievous bodily harm, since when he has been confined to a mental hospital and may never be released. So ended a determined police investigation into the brutal killing of an old lady in her garden, an investigation ultimately thwarted by the reluctance to testify by someone who saw what happened.

The Verdict

Without a trace of evidence at the scene of the murder, without the benefit of witnesses and being unable to trace stolen property, some of which even the victim's relatives were not able to describe, one must ask if there was any other route the police could have taken to detect this abominable crime. There was, and they took it: they sought and found the answer by identifying someone who was there, a reluctant witness who said so much, but nothing at all when it mattered, in a court of law.

The police had grounds to arrest and charge suspects, but not enough to pursue to conviction. If a case must be proved 'beyond reasonable doubt', as it must, it is hard to imagine how this is possible when a solitary witness remains mute and there is no other supportive evidence. Two persons were charged but did not face trial. The police, as they say, are not looking for anyone else.

Furneux Pelham 2004

Murder without Motive?

'Motive' and 'murder' have long been synonymous, the first usually providing the reason for the second. Most murders are detectable within a short period of time, the motive being obvious to investigating detectives whose job it is to prove the facts and let the motive speak for itself. Motive, however, becomes crucial when the killer is not known. 'Motive' is certainly a mystery regarding the killing of 83-year-old Robert Riley Workman at Furneux Pelham on 7th January, 2004.

Consider. Mr Workman, a retired Lieutenant-Colonel with the Royal Green Jackets, had lived at Cock House in this 'quintessential' Hertfordshire village for 27 years. He had shared the cottage with his wife, who had been ill for many years and who died the previous spring. There were no children of the marriage, and his wife's sister had also passed away. Alone in the world, save for an elderly brother, who emigrated to Australia 54 years before, and some distant relatives, Colonel Workman mainly kept himself to himself. Once a week he visited the local pub, the Brewery Tap, and the Post Office in nearby Braughing. 'Courteous, quiet and respectable', he was an old man living out his days in quiet retirement. Until, that is, that January evening when someone knocked on his front door.

It was about 8.15 p.m. One can imagine the scene, as Mr Workman, who was arthritic, responded to the caller's knock. As he opened the door to the darkness of a winter's night he was shot in the chest and died almost instantly, killed by buckshot discharged from a 12-bore shotgun, wounds that were certainly not self inflicted. The sound of the gun being discharged was heard by villagers, who would have thought it likely to be someone shooting pheasants or rabbits. Mr Workman lay where he fell, undisturbed until seven o'clock the next morning when his carer called at the cottage. Even so, neither she

Riley Workman

nor the GP, nor the police or ambulance crew who attended, realised Mr Workman had been shot. He was an old man who had apparently passed away, a heart attack probably. The body was covered with a duvet, and it was not until 10.10 a.m., when the undertakers arrived to remove it, that the grim truth was discovered. A delay of some three hours, during which several pairs of feet would have trampled over what was a crime scene. In any event no shotgun cartridge or any other clue was discovered.

Yet the killer may have been the same person who, at 4.57 the following morning, called 999 from a telephone kiosk at Braughing, requesting an ambulance attend 'Hollyhock Cottage, Furneux Pelham'. He was described as male, with the voice of someone aged 50–60 years, speaking with a 'rural' accent. When asked to spell the name of the village, the caller spelt it as 'Furneaux', with an 'a'. (The name is pronounced 'Furnix'). Two important points emerge from this: one, Hollyhock was Mrs Workman's preferred name of the cottage, and had indeed been its name around 1980 (after her favourite flower); and two, Furneux or Furneaux, is, or was, spelt both ways on separate signs in the village. Was the caller local, and did he know the Workman family?

An ambulance was dispatched to the village. The crew were unable to locate what they were told was Hollyhock Cottage and so drove off again. Then came the grim discovery, the subsequent attendance of the police – and the need to identify 'motive'. Who would turn up with a shotgun and shoot an old man dead, and why? The crime was premeditated. It shocked a community, and then the whole country as the details appeared in the national press and on television, including *Crimewatch*. So, what could the motive have been?

Theft? It seems nothing was stolen from the house, including some valuable silver. Mistaken identity? Possibly. A District Judge with the same surname may have been the target. There is no way of knowing. A grudge? Something or someone from Colonel Workman's past? He graduated from Oxford and joined the army, serving in the Far East during the War, and later as aide-de-camp to Field Marshall Slim. In 1965 he went into the antiques business, then got married. He and his wife came to live at Furneux Pelham. Colonel Workman's legacy was almost a million pounds, including the cottage, the beneficiaries being his brother and a nephew and niece, all resident in Australia, and some nephews and nieces on his wife's side. Suspects all, presumably. Likely to turn up on a winter's night and shoot the Colonel dead, hardly.

Not surprisingly, a 'sense of fear' prevailed in Furneux Pelham. Police offered panic alarms to residents (forty were accepted). A meeting was held in the village hall, chaired by Chief Superintendent Andy Wright. 'The purpose of the meeting was to reassure the community, but we did consider the murderer himself might have attended.' As well as identifying the killer, police sought to identify the 999 caller. Although probably one and the same person, there was a possibility the caller was someone else, someone who knew what had happened and sent for an ambulance. The tape recorded message was played twice at the meeting. No-one could identify the voice. An old man spent the last eight years of his life nursing his paralysed wife until she died, before he was shot down in the doorway of his home. A callous crime. A wicked crime. Perhaps someone will yet throw some light on the events that took place in a rural Hertfordshire village that evening, and provide the motive, so lacking to date. Someone from the distant past, perhaps. Or maybe someone not too far away. Who knows?

Riley Workman in his army days

*"If we are to abolish the death penalty,
let murderers take the first step"*

Alphonse Karr, 1808–90

Crime and Punishment

Was he right, then, Monsieur Karr, when he said, in effect, that capital punishment should be abolished only when murderers stopped committing murder? There is little doubt that most people in this country, if asked, would opt for its reintroduction. Who could blame them for seeking the ultimate retribution when they read of the most dreadful crimes imaginable. Armed robbers and rapists who kill; poisoners, such as Graham Young; those who kidnap and murder their victims.

To hang or not to hang.

There was a time, and not so long ago, when you could hang for what, by modern day standards, were relatively minor crimes. In 1817, 18-year-old William Moles paid the ultimate penalty for setting fire to a stack of wheat, with the unintentional consequences of damage to a farmer's property. Seen as justice then (by the favoured few who administered the law), hardly now. Today, we've moved on. But would hanging murderers do any good? Would it deter them? Would it be justice?

Most murders are 'domestic', that is to say offender and victim are acquainted. Most are born of some spontaneous act; many are caused through drunkenness (which is no excuse). Few are premeditated. If they were going to have capital punishment, the 1957 Homicide Act seemed to get things about right. The Act abolished the death penalty, save in the following circumstances:

Murder committed in the course of or furtherance of theft

Murder by shooting or explosion

Murder whilst resisting arrest or trying to escape

Murder of a police or prison officer

Two murders committed on two separate occasions.

At first glance this looks fair. On closer inspection it is flawed. The man who kills and steals one penny will hang; he who rapes and kills will not.

Hanging as a deterrent, then. If you kill you will hang. Would this prevent tragedies such as the murder of children, or killing the victim of a sexual attack to avoid identification? When the death penalty existed people committed murder. After it was abolished people committed murder. Capital punishment is hardly a deterrent. Many believe the murder rate increased, post abolition. It seems there is no way of telling, but you can forget statistics as a measure. Statistics are contrived, usually to prove or disprove some pre-supposed idea to fit the latest agenda. Hanging as a suitable punishment? An eye for an eye, as they say. Each of us must hold our own views. Personally I consider putting a rope around someone's neck and pulling a lever so that they drop through a trapdoor and suffocate is barbaric. (As is death by lethal injection, gas, electricity; none of them humane, and none as 'efficient' as hanging). Some murderers deserve it, so you might say; and murder is barbaric too, after all. But there is another reason why hanging can never be reintroduced. Quite simply, the criminal justice system is a game of chance. Detectives must investigate crime against the clock, and the rules are weighted against those who give their best endeavours to acquire a conviction. Consequently things can go wrong. No-one ever made a good job of anything when pressed for time to complete it. Barristers pit their wits against each other, each seeking to win, which is not the same as seeking justice. There may be doubt, and there is always the danger of the wrong conviction. Remember: once someone is hanged, they cannot be brought back to life.

Here, in these pages, are some cases where, in the view of the author, the perpetrators were wrongfully hanged. Did 'Silly Old' Mary Ansell really plot and scheme the death of her sister unaided, or was she in reality someone clearly lacking in intelligence who was motivated by someone else, someone aiming for a tidy profit through a life insurance claim? Was she guilty of murder, or simply a pawn in someone else's game? Charles Coleman was mad, surely. Should he have hanged, or should he have been locked up years before he killed Rose Gurney? Only people who are sane are accountable for their actions. Take Graham Young, a monster who murdered his workmates. Young escaped the noose only because hanging had been abolished. Was he really sane? (And did those who free him possess common sense?)

There are those who, nonetheless, deserved to be hanged. Those wicked brothers who kidnapped and murdered Muriel McKay, for example. Did they really deserve to live after what they did? David Lashley, and 'Mr X', who raped and murdered their young women victims: did they have any right to live, in the case of 'Mr X' if he had not taken his own life? Those armed robbers who shot Frank Mason — all three of them — did they deserve to live afterwards? Let's face it, none deserved the right to life after their wicked crimes. But society has no right to take life, not until the criminal justice system, such as it is, is failsafe, and it is certain that there cannot be a wrong conviction. That is a day that will never dawn.

We should be clear: for those who commit 'ordinary' crimes, such as burglary and theft, and many categories of assaults (insofar as 'ordinary' can be ordinary), there should always be, and is, a rehabilitation process in place to cater for ultimate release from prison. After all, prison should be about more than punishment. But for murder and other serious crimes, what should the punishment be?

Imprisonment for life is the sentence for murder, and would be more of a deterrent if the sentence meant what it said. Life should mean life, save in the most exceptional circumstances, of which for murder there should be few. Life imprisonment, where imposed for the more serious rape and robbery offences, should mean life too. Never mind release for 'good behaviour'. Graham Young was in the 'good behaviour' league, regarded as 'a model prisoner, eager to assist with his rehabilitation'. Of course he was: he wanted to be free, and when he was he killed again. Poisoners should never be released. Nor should terrorists. They who would kill with knives and guns, they who would strike down and kill an old lady in her own garden, and paedophiles who murder innocents, they should be put where they belong and kept there – in prison.

The Last to Hang

Gwynne Owen Evans (left) and Peter Anthony Allen were hanged at the same time, 8am, 13th August, 1964, at different locations, for the murder of a man at Workington, Cumbria. Evans was hanged at Strangeways prison, Manchester; Allen was hanged at Walton Prison, Liverpool. These were the last lawful executions in this country.

John Gootheridge's grave, Codicote churchyard
'Reburied a week later' after being stolen by bodysnatchers

BIBLIOGRAPHY

NEWSPAPERS & MAGAZINES
Berkhamsted Times
Hertfordshire Mercury
Illustrated London News
The Herts Advertiser and St Albans Times
Hertfordshire Countryside
The Watford Observer
The Herts Leader
The Watford Critic
The Historian
The Herts Leader
The West Herts & Watford Observer
Evening Standard (London)
Hemel Hempstead Gazette
Hatfield & Potters Bar Gazette
Welwyn & Hatfield Times
The Times
Medico-Legal Journal
The Daily Telegraph
Daily Express
Daily Mail
Evening News (London)
The Guardian
The Herald (Hemel Hempstead)

The author wishes to thank staff at Hertfordshire Archives and Library Service, County Hall, Hertford, and staff at Hertfordshire libraries who assisted with the research required to produce this book. Special acknowledgement is given to Pauline Sidell, Archivist, Dacorum Borough Council, as well as editorial staff of *The Watford Observer*, *The Hemel Hempstead Gazette*, *The Hertfordshire Mercury* and *The Hertfordshire Advertiser & St Albans Times*, and all publications from which material was gathered.

Special thanks to former colleagues of the Hertfordshire Constabulary, who kindly provided valuable information appertaining to specific chapters.

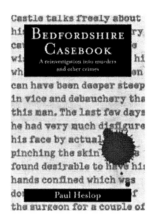

BEDFORDSHIRE CASEBOOK
A reinvestigation into murders and other crimes

Paul Heslop

This is a book about crime and punishment in Bedfordshire. It focuses mainly on the time when perpetrators were hanged for murder and lesser crimes, or sentenced to hard labour, or transported abroad for what today would be regarded as minor offences.

They range from the 17th century incarceration of John Bunyan, whose 'crime' was to preach outwith the established church; to rape and terror perpetrated by the man they called The Fox, on the South Bedfordshire borders in the 1980s. 'Domestic violence' features: the brutal murder of his wife by Joseph Castle in Luton in 1859, and the murder of 23-year-old Ruby Annie Keen at Leighton Buzzard by Leslie George Stone in 1937. We have the murder of Old Sally Marshall, at Little Staughton, in 1870; a Luton mugging that ended up as murder when William Worsley, convicted on the evidence of an accomplice, was hanged; and the A6 murder at Deadman's Hill, the infamous Hanratty case, still topical today.

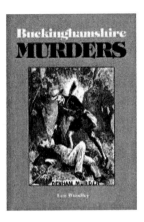  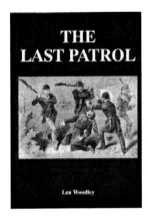

BUCKINGHAMSHIRE MURDERS   DEADLY DEEDS!
THE LAST PATROL

Three books by Len Woodley each dealing with murder

Buckinghamshire Murders contains thoroughly researched accounts of seventeen murders ranging across the old county of Buckinghamshire. Commencing from the early nineteenth century right up to modern times. Amongst others you will read about the Newton Longville shop-keeper murdered for a few shillings; the Dagnall killer; murders for no apparent reason at Buckingham and Denham; the unsolved murder of the canal man at Slough; love affairs that went tragically wrong at Burnham and Bourne End; a fatal ambush at Botolph Claydon.

Deadly Deeds includes accounts of fourteen murders that have occurred within the county of Buckinghamshire, plus one from central Europe. You will read about the Victorian 'Quaker' who, having escaped the gallows once, faced them again some years later; the country squire killed walking home from church; the gypsy who robbed and killed an old man, and the husband who shot his wife and her lover in one county, was tried in another and executed in yet another.

The Last Patrol details Policemen killed on duty by a criminal act within the area now covered by the Thames Valley Police – namely the counties of Berkshire, Buckinghamshire and Oxfordshire. These Police officers all started on their last day of duty as though they were going out on normal Police work, not one gave a thought to the possibility that he might be involved in, or sent to, a life-threatening job.

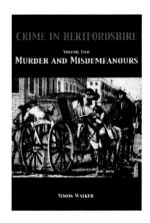

CRIME IN HERTFORDSHIRE
Volume One: Law and Disorder
Volume Two: Murders and Misdemeanours

Simon Walker

Volume One covers the history of law and order in Hertfordshire from the Anglo Saxon period to the middle of the twentieth century. Criminal law, the courts, the punishments and the means of enforcement have changed over the course of more than a thousand years, and the author traces those changes, illustrated with examples drawn from throughout Hertfordshire.

Volume Two is a collection of detailed accounts of crimes drawn from across the county, from 1602 to 1939. Locations include Hatfield, Hemel Hempstead, Hoddesdon, Berkhamsted, St.Albans, Ware, Hitchin, Datchworth and Bishops Stortford – some of the incidents may be familiar, most will be new to the reader. The rape of Maria Wells by her own father, and the publicity given to her testimony in court, was a tragedy for all concerned. Did Jane Norcott commit suicide, or was it murder? Why did Mary Boddy stab five-year-old George Hitch?

But it is more than just a collection of bloody crime; it provides an insight into the way that many of our Hertfordshire forebears lived their lives.

HAUNTED HERTFORDSHIRE
A Ghostly Gazetteer

Nicholas Connell and Ruth Stratton

The most extensive collection of the county's ghosts ever written, with over 300 stories. Many are little-known and previously unpublished, having been hidden away in the vaults of Hertfordshire Archives and Local Studies. Others are up to the moment accounts of modern hauntings in the words of those who have experienced them. All supported by dozens of rare and evocative pictures, an outline of the latest theories and diary dates of regular apparition appearances.

Stories feature a feast of phantoms, including grey ladies, dashing cavaliers, spectral transport, headless horsemen and a gallery of Kings and Queens.

Locations include Bishops Stortford, Datchworth, Harpenden, Hertford, Hitchin, Hoddeson, St. Albans, Ware and Watford.

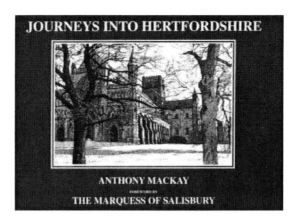

JOURNEYS INTO HERTFORDSHIRE

Anthony Mackay

This collection of nearly 200 ink drawings depicts the buildings and landscape of the still predominantly rural county of Hertfordshire. After four years of searching, the author presents his personal choice of memorable images, capturing the delights of a hitherto relatively unfeted part of England.

The area is rich in subtle contrasts – from the steep, wooded slopes of the Chilterns to the wide-open spaces of the north-east and the urban fringes of London in the south. Ancient market towns, an impressive cathedral city and countless small villages are surrounded by an intimate landscape of rolling farmland.

The drawings range widely over all manner of dwellings from stately home to simple cottage and cover ecclesiastical buildings from cathedral to parish church. They portray bridges, mills and farmsteads, chalk downs and watery river valleys, busy street scenes and secluded village byways.

The accompanying notes are deliberately concise but serve to entice readers to make their own journeys around this charming county.

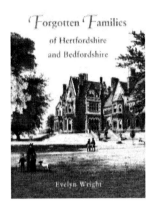

FORGOTTEN FAMILIES
of Hertfordshire and Bedfordshire

Evelyn Wright

This book tells the story of families once famous but whose fame is now mainly forgotten. They all lived in Hertfordshire and Bedfordshire in the 16th and 17th centuries, and include the Bechers of Renhold (of Becher's Brook fame), the Mordaunts of Turvey Abbey, Lady Cathcart of Tewin, the Bull family of Hertford, the Nodes family of Stevenage, the Docuras of Lilley and the Wicked Lady of Markyate Cell. All the families were related to each other, forming an intricate network over two counties: Hertfordshire and Bedfordshire. The author is one of their 20th century descendants. The book includes pedigrees showing the relationship between various families, and illustrations of many of the manor houses and mansions in which they lived.

Evelyn Wright was born in the village of Wingfield in Suffolk, and moved to Bedfordshire soon after her marriage in 1952. During a busy life bringing up five children, running a Nursery School and looking after elderly parents, she has always found time for writing. Evelyn is married to John Wright, a Chartered Surveyor, and they live in Aspley Heath in Bedfordshire.

THE HERTFORDSHIRE WAY
A waymarked long-distance footpath

Bert Richardson

This is a walkers' guidebook to the Hertfordshire Way, a 190-mile long-distance route on public rights-of-way around Hertfordshire. The book is divided into chapters, each representing a comfortable day's walk of 11 to 15 miles. Each chapter contains a detailed description of that part of the route with a two-colour map to assist the walker, and brief notes on significant features of the landscape together with several illustrations. The book is a completely new edition of the guidebook first published in 1998 (and now out of print). All the text has been revised to take account of changes in the route, the maps have been redrawn, most of the illustrations are new, there are two new chapters covering extensions to the route, a distance chart has been included and supporting information on public transport has been updated.

The Hertfordshire Way is a fully waymarked route providing access to much of the County's very attractive countryside. Starting points for eight of the sixteen 'legs' are on main railway lines out of London, making this an easily accessible route for walkers from the Capital as well as those in Hertfordshire and neighbouring counties.

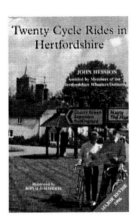

TWENTY CYCLE RIDES IN HERTFORDSHIRE

John Hession
Assisted by members of the Hertfordshire Wheelers/Dobsons

John Hession's book is the key to the discovery of the many varied delights of the Hertfordshire countryside, much of it just few miles from the dense outer-suburbs of London. At the same time encouraging gentle exercise and enjoying clean country air.

It enables you to find the hidden Hertfordshire of ancient village greens, country houses and pubs, the rolling landscape of the Chiltern's lower slopes, the varied pattern of fields, woodlands and winding lanes. All seemingly miles from the noise and commotion of motorways, trunk roads and town life. The atmosphere of the county is beautifully captured too in the sketches by the well-known artist Ronald Maddox which appear throughout the book.

Starting points for the rides, which vary from 15 to 36 miles, are all at railway stations so that visitors from outside the county, or who live in another part, have ready access.

211

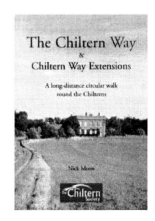

THE CHILTERN WAY
A 200km circular walk round the Chilterns

Nick Moon

This book is a guide to the original circular long distance path through Bedfordshire, Buckinghamshire, Hertfordshire & Oxfordshire.

The Chiltern Way was established by the Chiltern Society to mark the Millennium by providing walkers in the twenty-first century with a new way of exploring the diverse, beautiful countryside which all four Chiltern counties have to offer. Based on the idea of the late Jimmy Parson's Chiltern Hundred but expanded to cover the whole Chilterns, the route has been designed by the author and has been signposted, waymarked and improved by the Society's Rights of Way Group.

This guide includes 29 specially drawn maps of the route indicating points of interest, local pubs, car parks, railway stations and a skeleton road network and details are provided of the Ordnance Survey and Chiltern Society maps covering the route.

THE CHILTERN WAY & CHILTERN WAY EXTENSIONS
A long-distance circular walk round the Chilterns

Nick Moon

This is the new complete official guide to the now extended circular long-distance path through Bedfordshire, Buckinghamshire, Hertfordshire and Oxfordshire, whereby the society has responded to demand by incorporating further mileage both to the north and to the south of the original route.

CHILTERN WALKS
Hertfordshire, Bedfordshire and North Buckinghamshire

Nick Moon

One of a series of three books providing a comprehensive coverage of walks throughout the whole of the Chiltern area (as defined by the Chiltern Society). The walks included vary in length from 3.0 to 10.9 miles, but are mainly in the 5–7 mile range popular for half-day walks, although suggestions of possible combinations of walks are given for those preferring a full day's walk.

Each walk gives details of nearby places of interest and is accompanied by a specially drawn map of the route which also indicates local pubs and a skeleton road network.

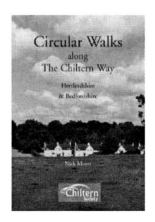

CIRCULAR WALKS ALONG THE CHILTERN WAY
Volume Two   Hertfordshire & Bedfordshire

Nick Moon

The second of a two-volume series with special maps provided for each walk.

The walks range from 4.3 to 8.8 miles which makes for a comfortable half day or a leisurely full day walk. In addition, details of several possible combinations of walks of up to 22 miles are provided for those who would like a longer, more challenging walk.

Each walk gives details of nearby places of interest and is accompanied by a specially drawn map of the route which also indicates local pubs and a skeleton road network.

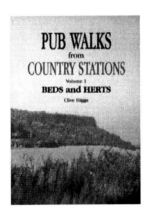

PUB WALKS FROM COUNTRY STATIONS:
Volume 1   Beds and Herts

Clive Higgs

One of two titles both containing fourteen circular country rambles, each starting and finishing at a railway station and incorporating a pub-stop at a mid-way point.

Volume 1 has 5 walks in Bedfordshire starting from Sandy, Biggleswade, Harlington, Flitwick and Linslade. Together with 9 walks in Hertfordshire starting from Watford, Kings Langley, Boxmoor, Berkhamsted, Tring, Stanstead St.Margaret's, Watton-at-Stone, Bricket Wood and Harpenden.

The shortest walk is a distance of 4miles and the longest 7 and a half miles.

FAMILY WALKS
Chilterns – South

Nick Moon

One in a series of two books, providing a comprehensive coverage of walks throughout the whole of the Chiltern area. The walks included vary in length from 1.7 to 5.5 miles, but are mainly in the 3 to 5 mile range, which is ideal for families with children, less experienced walkers or short winter afternoons.

Each walk text gives details of nearby places of interest and is accompanied by a specially drawn map of the route, which also indicates local pubs and a skeleton road network.

The author, Nick Moon, has lived in or regularly visited the Chilterns all his life and has for 25 years, been an active member of the Chiltern Society's Rights of Way Group, which seeks to protect and improve the area's footpath and bridleway network.